# Rock TOPICON

*UNLIKELY QUESTIONS AND THEIR SURPRISING ANSWERS*

## DAVE MARSH, SANDRA CHORON & DEBBIE GELLER

Contemporary Books, Inc.
Chicago

**Library of Congress Cataloging in Publication Data**

Marsh, Dave.
  Rocktopicon.

  Includes index.
  1. Rock music—History and criticism.   I. Choron,
Sandra.   II. Geller, Debbie.   III. Title.
ML3534.M4     1984       784.5'4       84-14935
ISBN 0-8092-5474-3

All photographs are from the collection of Peter Kanze.

Published by Contemporary Books, Inc.
180 North Michigan Avenue, Chicago, Illinois 60601
Manufactured in the United States of America
Library of Congress Catalog Card Number: 84-14935
International Standard Book Number: 0-8092-5474-3

Published simultaneously in Canada by Beaverbooks, Ltd.
195 Allstate Parkway, Valleywood Business Park
Markham, Ontario L3R 4T8 Canada

For the ones who got away

# Contents

# *Acknowledgments*

For sharing their time, talents, good humor, and records, *Rocktopicon* owes a debt to many, and we welcome the opportunity to thank them here.

For understanding from the start that all trivia is not trivial, and for his textual contributions, we thank Rick Vittenson, formerly of Contemporary Books. Thanks, too, to Kathy Willhoite for seeing us through.

For contributing their favorite bits of rock & roll minutiae, thanks to Greil Marcus, John Tobler, Wayne King, Lee Ballinger, Carrie Ballinger, Steve Futterman, Alan Jones, Tom Hibbert, Mark Williams, and especially to Mike Callahan. Fran Pelzman's research facilities, extensive record collection, and generosity were also helpful, as were the facilities of Bleecker Bob's in New York City and Igor's Records in Teaneck, New Jersey. And we owe a debt (it's in the mail) to Peter Kanze for all the photographs herein.

Harry Choron's fact-checking efforts and general support proved invaluable, as did those of our title consultant, Alan Novich.

Finally, a special tip of the hat to Jim Nettleton for going to the library with Debbie and telling funny jokes when they were supposed to be quiet.

# *Introduction*

You could call *Rocktopicon* a trivia book. It has the format and required amount of recondite information. But there's a catch that makes this trivia book different from all the rest. The information you'll receive in the answers is trivial only at first glance. If this were a more just world (by which we mean one in which Gene Vincent and Brian Holland were as much household names as, say, Merv Griffin and Duran Duran), all of the facts we've included here would be understood as essential—or, at least, significant.

That is not to say that *Rocktopicon* does not contain a great many fairly obscure facts. Actually, it is so full of them that we hope to stump dedicated rock fans and hardcore trivia buffs as well as more casual readers and listeners. But the out-of-the-way facts assembled here aren't a dead end. In our judgment, knowing that it was "The Girl From Ipanema" that won the Grammy for Record of the Year in 1964 instead of, say, "I Want to Hold Your Hand" or "She Loves You," both of which were released that same year, lends an insight into some of rock's finest moments and the way in which they were perceived by the music establishment. Similarly, knowing who recorded the original version of "Ruby Baby" adds something to your knowledge of rock history and perhaps helps you to make some important connections between Dion (who made the best-known version of the song) and the Drifters (who started it off). At the very least, it's something to chew over—or, if you're enthusiastic enough, a great excuse to go out and hear some of the two or three thousand great records made over the past thirty years. It is our hope that along the way, our collection of unlikely questions and their surprising answers will comprise a fascinating guide to the journey.

One of the wonders of rock & roll is that no one has heard it all; there's no orderly library in which it's all contained, no system for teaching ourselves about it. And that's the fun of the thing. Hopefully, *Rocktopicon* provides an amusing, entertaining, and enlightening method for learning not only more facts but new ways of looking at what seems to be inconsequential. Because if there's one thing rock has taught us, simply by sticking around all these years, it's that what seems to be ain't necessarily so.

That's really what this book is all about.

—Dave Marsh, March 1984

# 1

# In The Beginning There Was Nothing But Rock . . .
## (Rock & Roll Before Elvis)

1. Alan Freed, whose radio programs in Cleveland and New York have resulted in his being generally acknowledged as the "Father of Rock & Roll," was using the term "rock & roll" to refer to the types of music he played on his shows in the early and mid-1950s. But Freed didn't invent the term out of thin air, as some would later claim. What are the origins of the term?

2. Arthur "Big Boy" Crudup recorded for RCA as a blues singer during the period 1941–56. During that time he recorded two songs that would have a big influence on what was later to become rock & roll. What were the songs, and why were they important?

1. Freed certainly made the term popular, and it's unlikely that we would be calling this style of music "rock & roll" were it not for him. But both the terms "rock" and "roll" were well-known in the forties and even earlier, and were sexually suggestive. In the late 1940s Wild Bill Moore recorded a tune called "Rock and Roll," as did Joe Haymes in 1935. Neither would be considered rock & roll by today's standards, but they do prove that the term was kicking around considerably earlier than when Freed used it.

Alan Freed with Dean Barlow, 1955. If Barlow was passing anything under the table, it didn't do much good—he never had anything approaching a pop hit.

2. Elvis Presley was a big Crudup fan and recorded "That's All Right Mama" in his first professional session, although Elvis's version only slightly resembles the original. Presley's version had a great influence on rock & roll due to his unexpected success with the song in Memphis. Presley later hit the national charts with another Crudup song, "My Baby Left Me," which he recorded essentially unchanged from the Crudup version.

3. *In the early 1950s R&B, popular ("pop") music, and C&W (country and western) music were widely different from one another in terms of their sounds, audiences, and sales. Rarely did R&B or C&W songs sell enough records to "cross over" into the national best-seller (pop) charts, largely because record shops and radio stations were segregated. While Northern white singers often had pop hits with their versions of R&B tunes, one of the earliest, if not the earliest, R&B crossovers from a pre-rock & roll group occurred in 1951. What was the song, what was the group, and why was the group important to rock & roll?*

---

4. *What characteristic is shared by such rock staples as "Going Up the Country" (Canned Heat), "Corrine, Corrina" (Joe Turner, Bob Dylan, Ray Peterson), "Prodigal Son" (the Rolling Stones), and "Walk Right In" (the Rooftop Singers)?*

---

5. *Why was Dave Bartholomew important to early rock & roll? What record did he make in 1951 that became a national number 1 hit for another rock & roller more than twenty years later?*

3. The song was "60 Minute Man," by the Dominoes. Although the lyric was suggestive enough to get the song banned from virtually every pop radio station, it was such a runaway R&B hit (seven *months* on the Top 10 R&B charts, including fourteen weeks at number 1) that it actually crashed the national pop Top 30 for four weeks. The group, led by Billy Ward, featured a singer named Clyde McPhatter, who was later replaced by Jackie Wilson. Both McPhatter and Wilson were later central figures in rock & roll.

4. They're all based on black blues records made in the 1920s. "Going Up the Country" is a version of "Bull Doze Blues" by Henry Thomas (1928); it even has the same intro. "Corrine, Corrina" was done in the same year by Bo Carter and is a staple of many blues singers' repertoires. "Prodigal Son" is the 1929 Robert Wilkins song "That's No Way to Get Along." "Walk Right In" was done in 1929 by Cannon's Jug Stompers. If you think rock & roll sprang out of nowhere, find a copy of the LP *Roots of Rock* (Yazoo 1063, released in 1978) and try not to be too shocked by what you hear.

5. Bartholomew was a bandleader from New Orleans who worked with Fats Domino during the early parts of Domino's career. Bartholomew's band is heard not only on virtually every early Fats Domino record, but also on scores of other well-known early rock & roll records by later stars such as Little Richard and Lloyd Price. In 1951 Bartholomew released "My Ding-a-Ling" (King Records), a song that his band played in clubs, with the band and the crowd making up verses as they went along. Chuck Berry used lyrics similar to those on Bartholomew's 1951 record in making his live version of the song a number 1 hit in 1972. Times change, but Berry's version was still banned by many stations for being too suggestive in 1972, twenty-one years after Bartholomew had run into the same problem.

6. *Shirley Gunter, lead singer of the Queens, had a Top 10 R&B hit in 1954 with an early rock & roll song called "Oop Shoop." This was the Queens' only national hit. Both Shirley's brother and another female member of the Queens went on to surpass her successes, as members of other groups closely associated with early rock & roll. Who were they, and what were the groups?*

7. *Among the songs tossed around as being "the first rock & roll song" (which, we might add, will never be agreed upon and probably doesn't exist), "Sh-Boom" by the Chords ranks highly. Hitting the charts in mid-1954, it was "covered" (copied for white audiences) by the Crew Cuts but still managed to sell well enough to place in the national Top 10 pop charts. One well-known television personality of that time was furious that the record by the Chords did well and worried about it setting a precedent. Who was he, and what did he do about it?*

8. *In 1951 a little-known country & western singer covered a rhythm & blues record, "Rocket 88," for C&W audiences. The record was a flop, but it was an interesting experiment for the country singer, who at one time had been a yodeler with aspirations to the American yodeling championship. In 1951 he was working at a radio station in Chester, Pennsylvania. The next year, he recorded the theme song of the R&B program that aired before his country show, and achieved mild success. The yodeler continued recording rhythm & blues songs in his country style, including a song originally done by Sonny Dae and His Knights which the country singer turned into a rock & roll anthem. Who was he, and what were the songs?*

6.   Shirley's brother was Cornelius Gunter, who sang for a time in the Coasters, among other groups. And Zola Taylor of the Queens went on to a lengthy career with the Platters, racking up hit after hit in the late 1950s. Zola also sang lead on the 1957 hit "He's Mine."

7.   The TV personality was Stan Freberg, a notorious rock & roll hater. Freberg thought the Chords' record was moronic and poorly produced, and he cut a parody of the song for Capitol in which he made fun of singers mumbling, threatening to fire the singer for letting words be understood, and the like. Freberg also took shots at other rock & roll records in parodies of such songs as Presley's "Heartbreak Hotel" and the Platters' "The Great Pretender." To prove he wasn't one-dimensional, he also made fun of Harry Belafonte, Mitch Miller, and Lawrence Welk. Maybe he just hated everybody.

8.   The theme from the R&B show was "Rock the Joint," recorded on the Essex label by Bill Haley and the Saddlemen. Thinking that the name Saddlemen was a bit too country, Haley began calling his group the Comets and had several successes (the biggest being "Shake, Rattle and Roll," the Joe Turner R&B tune) before he recorded the Sonny Dae tune in 1954. The record went nowhere until it was featured in 1955 in the motion picture *The Blackboard Jungle*, whereupon it became a monster hit. The song was "(We're Gonna) Rock around the Clock," by Bill Haley and His Comets.

9.  In the early 1950s pianist Willie Perryman from Atlanta was using a style of boogie piano that was not unlike what later would sound quite at home in rock & roll. He had several R&B chart records under his stage name, then disappeared from the national charts until 1962, when he had two more hits under a different stage name. To demonstrate that his boogie style was compatible with rock & roll, he recorded one of his 1951 hits in essentially the same style, and it became a hit in 1962. What were his stage names, what was the double hit, and which of his songs did the Beatles record?

10. In the mid-1950s a hairdresser from St. Louis was undecided whether to pursue music or cosmetology as a career. After receiving encouragement from Muddy Waters, he decided to take up music full time. His first recording was a song he had written called "Ida Red." When the recording was issued in 1955 the title and lyrics were changed slightly and the song became a rock & roll classic. What was the song, and who was the erstwhile hairdresser?

11. In early 1955 Federal Records released a song by an un-known California-based R&B group under the guidance of a writer/manager whose experience dated back to the 1930s big bands of Duke Ellington, Count Basie, and the Dorseys. The record was an unmitigated flop. Undaunted, the manager made a deal with Mercury Records providing that he would sign another of his groups, who at that time had a big hit, only if Mercury would take the group with the Federal flop. The manager then had the group re-record the same song for Mercury, and it went on to become a million-seller. Who was the manager, what were the two groups involved, and what was the flop-turned-hit?

9. Willie Perryman was usually known as Piano Red. He had several hits for RCA under that name, including "Right String But the Wrong Yo-Yo," which he re-recorded under the name Dr. Feelgood and the Interns in 1962—it charted again. On the flipside of his first Okeh single as Dr. Feelgood, Perryman recorded "Mr. Moonlight," which the Beatles included on their LP *Beatles '65*.

10. Blues singer Muddy Waters suggested Chuck Berry go to Chicago to Chess Records with his song "Ida Red." The song metamorphosed into "Maybellene."

11. Federal Records had released "Only You (And You Alone)" by the Platters in early 1955 but, as indicated by its sales, the song wasn't very well performed. Manager Buck Ram (who also wrote "Only You") was negotiating with Mercury Records to sign his other client, the Penguins, who had just had a big hit with "Earth Angel ." In order to get the Penguins, Mercury also signed the Platters, who followed "Only You," a gold record, with literally dozens of additional chart sides. The Penguins never had another hit.

**12.** *Elvis Presley's appearance on television in early 1956 placed a nationwide spotlight on rock & roll. "Heartbreak Hotel" was the first Presley record on the national pop charts, but six months before, a country singer with a rock & roll style had begun putting hits on the national country charts. His first three records for the Sun label were no more than local or regional hits, but in 1955 his fourth record went to number 10 and his fifth to number 1 on the country charts. Although country music fans were well aware of this singer, the general public had never heard of him. Who was he?*

---

**13.** *When Clyde McPhatter left the Dominoes, he organized a group that would be part of the rock & roll scene for another decade, although its personnel changed repeatedly. When McPhatter was drafted in late 1954, his place as lead singer was taken part of the time by a singer who sounded somewhat like Clyde and who later had two chart hits of his own, "Itchy Twitchy Feeling" and "Psycho." What was the name of McPhatter's group, and who was his part-time stand-in?*

---

**14.** *When Tommy Edwards hit number 1 with "It's All in the Game" in 1958, many people thought the song sounded familiar. Why?*

12. Presley himself. Because of the way music was sold before rock & roll, it was rare that someone who listened and broadcast pop music ever heard country or R&B, and vice versa. When Elvis signed with RCA in 1955, that label began promoting him to pop audiences. In his 1956 TV appearance, Elvis was no surprise to most country music listeners, but to everybody else, Presley just sort of "appeared," with a fully developed style that was to most severely shocking.

---

13. The group was the Drifters. Over the years the group underwent many personnel changes but none so drastic as the one in 1959, when the entire group (which no longer included McPhatter) was fired by its manager, George Treadwell, who owned the group's name, and replaced by another group, the Five Crowns (which included Ben E. King).

   The "old" Drifters scored such hits as "Money Honey," "Drip Drop," and "Honey Love"; the new incarnation of the group began its hit career with "There Goes My Baby" and continued through the mid-1960s, with many further personnel changes—notably Rudy Lewis, who stepped in when King struck out on his own, and Johnny Moore.

   When McPhatter was in the Army in the mid-fifties, he was temporarily replaced by Bobby Hendricks. Hendricks's 1960 hit, "Psycho," had nothing to do with Alfred Hitchcock's movie, though the song was a first cousin of the later hit, "The Name Game," by Shirley Ellis.

---

14. Edwards had already had a hit with the same song, seven years earlier. Never one to miss a chance, Edwards re-recorded his other 1951 hit, "The Morning Side of the Mountain," in 1959, and it also hit again.

15. *Much has been written about white artists "covering" black artists' songs during the mid-1950s. One song, originally done in 1954 by a black group, the Jewels, was covered by the Fontane Sisters and reached number 1 on the pop charts. The same song was also covered by a black group, and this black cover version stands today as an early rock & roll classic. What was the song and the group? What other cover records was this group or its lead singer involved with?*

16. *In 1954 a group formerly known as the Royals made a name change and started a series of songs known as "The Annie Songs." Everyone seemed to be jumping on the "Annie" bandwagon, with the group reeling off three "Annie" hits, Etta James hitting with an answer song, and Georgia Gibbs cleaning up the Etta James tune for white audiences and the pop charts. Name the original three hits, the group, its lead singer, the Etta James song, and the retitled Georgia Gibbs song. For extra credit, what "Annie" song was done by Buddy Holly?*

**15.** The song was "Hearts of Stone"; the group was the Charms, with Otis Williams singing lead. The Charms made a career out of being involved with cover records one way or another. The follow-up to "Hearts of Stone" was "Ling, Ting, Tong," originally done by the Five Keys, while the Charms' own "Two Hearts" was covered by Pat Boone in 1955. The next year Otis Williams and Cathy Carr each competed with the Tin Pan Alley tune "Ivory Tower." Although both Williams's and Carr's versions came out virtually simultaneously, and so might both be considered "originals," the song was then covered by Gale Storm (TV's "My Little Margie"), whose version made the Top 10.

---

**16.** The Royals, then virtually unknown, changed their name to Hank Ballard and the Midnighters to avoid confusion with the well-known "5" Royales. The Midnighters first hit with "Work with Me Annie" in spring 1954, in which they pleaded, "Work with me Annie, let's get it while the gettin' is good . . ." Next they sang that "Annie Had a Baby" and couldn't work no more. They followed that with "Annie's Aunt Fannie," who kept a close eye on Annie. Etta James, in an answer song directed toward the Midnighters' lead singer, Hank (Henry) Ballard, released "The Wallflower" in early 1955, in which she invited "Roll with me, Henry." Georgia Gibbs covered the song but changed the title to "Dance with Me Henry (Wallflower)" and also removed most of the other sexual allusions. Gibbs's version made number 1 on the pop charts even as "Work with Me Annie" reached number 1 on the R&B charts.

Even Buddy Holly eventually did an "Annie" song, "Midnight Shift," in which he suggested that Annie had become a working girl, in the most ancient sense.

17. *In early 1955 Georgia Gibbs covered a rhythm & blues song by LaVern Baker and touched off a new controversy in the already touchy area of cover records. The new complaint was that Gibbs had copied the LaVern Baker record virtually note for note, arrangement and all. What was the record, and why were certain people concerned about cover records? How did rock & roll's prominence over the following two years resolve the cover record problem?*

17. The record, "Tweedle Dee," raised questions about music world ethics and racism. In the early 1950s the three main branches of music on records—popular, rhythm & blues, and country & western—were almost completely segregated. A hit in one category could never be heard by listeners of the other two categories, because radio stations, record stores, and jukeboxes were carefully stocked with only one style of music. As a result artists began recording material from other categories for their own markets. In the pop market, this was a long-standing practice that went back to the beginning of the twentieth century, when sellers of sheet music wanted to get as many performers as possible to sing their songs. With the coming to prominence of the R&B artists on one side, and country artists such as Presley on the other, pop artists found a trove of excellent material which pop audiences had never heard. The system's racism asserted itself when black and Southern performers—particularly black ones—couldn't get their records played on the pop stations, where the greatest sales potential was. When pop singers began copying country and R&B records note for note it became unavoidably clear that the only difference was the race of the artist.

Rock & roll achieved its greatest cultural breakthrough by eradicating the barriers separating the three categories of music. Once the pop audience was able to hear the originals, it almost always bought them instead of the copies. By 1958 the cover record practice was almost finished.

Interestingly enough, today's music scene is again similar to the early 1950s. Rock music is today's mainstream (as was pop), with country and soul (R&B's descendant) having almost totally different audiences as a result of air play segregation. What was once pop music in the 1950s has now become "adult contemporary" and represents a fourth category, although it is closely related to pop/rock. Cover records among the categories are still common today, with white pop singers cashing in more heavily than anyone else.

**18.**  *During the early and mid-1950s a vocal group from Washington, D.C., had hits on the R&B charts with such tunes as "Lovey Dovey," "One Mint Julep," "Devil or Angel," and "Blue Velvet," all of which would later be redone and appear on the pop charts as hits by others. What was the group, and what rock & roll classic did it hit with in the late 1950s? Bonus question: What rock & roll classic did the group update for the Aladdin label in 1975?*

---

**19.**  *In 1951 a young singer named Johnnie Ray released a record on the Okeh label that went to number 1 on the pop charts. The record achieved an unprecedented feat by also going to number 1 on the R&B charts. What was the record? What was unusual about Johnnie Ray's stage performances, and what nickname did these performances gain him?*

---

**20.**  *In 1956 Johnnie Ray had a big hit with a non-crying tune called "Just Walking in the Rain." What was unusual about the song's origin?*

18.  The group was the Clovers, whose Atlantic label recordings of the early 1950s were immensely popular with the R&B audience, giving them no less than fifteen songs in the Top 10 by 1956. Many of these Clovers songs became rock & roll hits. "Lovey Dovey" seems to have endured particularly well. For instance, some of that song's lyrics were included in the 1973 Steve Miller Band hit "The Joker." Miller even followed up with another Clovers song, "Your Cash Ain't Nothin' But Trash."

The Clovers also hit big in 1959 with "Love Potion No. 9," with which the Searchers, a British group, had a Top 10 hit in 1964.

In 1975 the group recorded "Bump Jive!" in their hometown, Washington. It was a remodeling of the Johnny Otis rock & roll hit "Willie and the Hand Jive," with disco-oriented lyrics.

19.  The song that was simultaneously number 1 on the pop and R&B charts, an extremely rare feat for a white singer, was "Cry." The flipside, "The Little White Cloud that Cried," was indicative of Ray's approach to music. For a time Ray's stage performances featured him virtually crying and bawling his way through shows, and bursting into tears became his trademark, earning him the nickname "The Prince of Wails."

20.  "Just Walking in the Rain" was written by members of a group called the Prisonaires, who were residing in the Tennessee State Penitentiary. The group had been assembled in prison by Johnny Bragg, who had been with various incarnations of the Prisonaires since the late 1940s. Bragg's Prisonaires were given a pass to go to Memphis and record for Sam Phillips's Sun label but then had to return to the slammer. The original version of "Just Walking in the Rain" appears on Sun 186.

16

21. In 1952 a group of kids in a New Orleans neighborhood pooled its resources, came up with about two dollars, and went to Cosimo's Recording Studio to try to record a song. Studio owner Cosimo Matassa recalls that it was the cheapest session he ever did and claims that the whole neighborhood was on the tape. A few months later, as Matassa was erasing surplus session tapes, he came across the kids' song and played it for a visiting record company executive. The exec liked two of the singers, a girl and a boy, and eventually signed them to his label, Aladdin. Who were they, and what was the song they were singing on the tape?

22. In the mid-1950s a pianist named Jack Fina recorded a classical piece in a boogie piano style for the Mercury label. In 1961 another artist, Kim Fowley, using an unlikely pseudonym, made the same arrangement of the song a rock & roll hit on the Rendezvous label. Name the song and artist on the Rendezvous hit.

23. In 1952 a young singer from Georgia recorded four songs for RCA, all of which went on to become resounding misses. The singer then joined the Tempo Toppers vocal group and sang on four records issued by Peacock. Again, no success. But his next record, released on a third label and as a solo artist, became a rock & roll classic, and the singer today is recognized as one of the founding fathers of rock & roll. Who was he, and what was the 1956 hit that propelled him to stardom?

21. The girl was Shirley Goodman and the boy was Leonard Lee, who at the time were only fourteen and fifteen years old, respectively. The song, which had many verses (Shirley has recalled, "It went on and on"), was slimmed down to what became the duo's first hit, "I'm Gone." Shirley and Lee became the Sweethearts of the Blues and rolled up such hits as "Feel So Good," "I Feel Good," and "Let the Good Times Roll." Later these songs would be redone by Johnny Preston, Bunny Sigler, and even Shirley and Lee themselves (they placed "Let the Good Times Roll" in the Top 50 in both 1956 and 1960). Shirley later hit on her own in 1975 with "Shame, Shame, Shame," a disco-oriented song that was credited to Shirley (and Company).

---

22. The song was "Bumble Boogie," based on Rimski-Korsakov's classic "The Flight of the Bumblebee." Fowley's group used the name B. Bumble and the Stingers. The B. Bumble hit was not very different at all from the Jack Fina original, illustrating how closely rock & roll used earlier styles such as boogie music. A decade later B. Bumble was itself copied when its second hit, "Nutrocker," was recorded by Emerson, Lake & Palmer.

---

23. He was Little Richard, and the song was "Tutti-Frutti." In the early 1950s Little Richard experimented with blues, boogie, and gospel styles on his RCA and Peacock sides. When he finally switched to Specialty in 1955, he had developed the wild, screaming style that endeared him to the rock & roll audience, and he went on to chart a long string of hits.

24. *McHouston Baker was one of the better-known session musicians of the early 1950s. In 1953 he played on the R&B hit "Mama, He Treats Your Daughter Mean" by Ruth Brown, which led to many other recording jobs. To help make ends meet, Baker tutored beginners and eventually even wrote an instruction book. In 1955 he decided to team up with one of his female students. The duo recorded one of the best remembered hits of the early rock era. By what name do we know McHouston Baker, who was his student, and what was their biggest hit?*

25. *A California-based rhythm & blues singer wrote and recorded a song in 1956 that has since become one of the definitive rock & roll standards. The singer appeared on many records in the 1950s, among them Etta James's "Wallflower" and Donald Woods's "Death of an Angel." Who was he, and on what memorable Robins disc did he do guest vocals?*

26. *What was the first record released on Sun Records?*

27. *In 1953 a young Brooklynite began winning Apollo Theater talent contests and soon made his first record, "Daddy Rollin' Stone." Later he became one of the most successful rock & roll songwriters of the 1950s. Who was he?*

24. McHouston Baker was better known as Mickey "Guitar" Baker. He teamed up with Sylvia Vanderpool to form Mickey and Sylvia. Their biggest hit was "Love Is Strange" in 1957. In 1973 Sylvia (now Robinson) had a solo hit with "Pillow Talk." Today she's the proprietor of Sugar Hill Records, where rap originated.

---

25. Richard Berry was one of R&B's first "session singers" in the 1950s. In addition to many records under his own name, he sang the bass part of "Wallflower" by Etta James and can be heard sobbing in the background of Donald Woods's "Death of an Angel." He did a guest vocal with the Robins on "Riot in Cell Block #9" and was a member of the Flares.

    Berry's biggest success, however, was as writer and original performer of "Louie Louie." In 1983 Rhino Records issued an entire album of versions of "Louie Louie." *The Best of Louie Louie* (Rhino, RNEP 065) includes Berry's initial recording plus several of those that made the song famous, including the Kingsmen's

---

26. The otherwise unmemorable "Drivin' Slow," by Johnny London, released on March 1, 1952.

---

27. Otis Blackwell was responsible for writing "Don't Be Cruel," "All Shook Up," "Return to Sender," and "One Broken Heart for Sale," all for Elvis; "Great Balls of Fire" and "Breathless" for Jerry Lee Lewis; "Fever" for Little Willie John (and Peggy Lee); "Hey Little Girl" for Dee Clark; "Handy Man" for Jimmy Jones; and many others. "Daddy Rolling Stone" was the B side of the Who's second single, "Anyway, Anyhow, Anywhere," in 1965.

♪ . ♪ . ♪ . ♪ . ♪ . ♪

**28.** *In the early 1950s one team wrote songs for many of the R&B stars of the time: Amos Milburn, Peppermint Harris, Bull-moose Jackson, Floyd Dixon, and the Robins, among others. In the late 1950s they were responsible for producing several excellent rock & roll hits—so many that the team is now an institution. Who were they, and which of their 1953 R&B hits later became one of Elvis Presley's signature tunes?*

**29.** *In 1948 this R&B bandleader opened the Barrelhouse Club in Los Angeles. Some of the acts he discovered or recorded with were Little Esther (Phillips), Jackie Wilson, Little Willie John, Hank Ballard, the Robins, and Johnny Ace. In 1958 he had a big rock & roll hit under his own name. Who was he?*

**30.** *Aaron and Art Neville are best known as the Neville Brothers or the Meters. (Under the latter designation they had the 1969 Top 40 hits "Sophisticated Cissy" and "Cissy Strut.") Aaron also scored on his own in 1967 with "Tell It Like It Is." In their hometown of New Orleans the Nevilles are also known as the leaders of a fifties harmony group and one of the city's leading Mardi Gras tribes. Name them.*

**31.** *In the mid-1950s a group called the Moonlighters recorded for Chess Records. They were indeed moonlighting, since they were also a successful early doo-wop group under another name. Who were they?*

28. Jerry Leiber and Mike Stoller were among the first indepen-
dent producers in rock & roll. They wrote the 1953 hit
"Hound Dog," which later became associated with Elvis
Presley. It was first an R&B hit for Willie Mae "Big Mama"
Thornton. Leiber and Stoller wrote and produced the Coas-
ters' hits and in the 1960s were responsible for many of the
Drifters' successes. They were also an influence on Phil
Spector, who was apprenticed to them in the early stages of
his production career.

29. Johnny Otis was unquestionably a major force in developing
the sound that evolved into rock & roll. "The Johnny Otis
Show," his R&B revue, toured extensively during the 1950s,
and during these tours he discovered many future rock &
roll stars. In 1958 Otis recorded a rock & roll classic, "Willie
and the Hand Jive."

30. The Hawkettes had several local discs in the fifties. Each
year at Mardi Gras the Nevilles get out their robes, feathers,
drums, and horns and go on parade as the Wild Tchoupitou-
las, who have recorded one album for Island.

31. The Moonlighters were actually the Moonglows, who had
hits with "Sincerely," "See Saw," and (under the name
Harvey and the Moonglows) "The Ten Commandments of
Love," all for Chess.

# 2

# ... And Then Things Just Started To Roll
## (Fifties Rock)

32. *In 1957 a singer from Texas wrote a song about a girl named Cindy Lou. The singer's drummer was dating a girl with a similar name, and the group decided to change the name of the song to hers. Who was the singer, what was the group, and under what title did the song become a hit?*

32. The singer was Buddy Holly, who did some records under his own name and used the name of the group, the Crickets, for others. Crickets drummer Jerry Allison was dating Peggy Sue, who gave the song its eventual title. Even though the Crickets were all on the hit record, only Buddy Holly's name was used. In real life, Allison and Peggy Sue eventually married, at which point Holly wrote a sequel, "Peggy Sue Got Married." Years later, after Holly's death, the Allisons divorced, but this event went unrecorded (or at least, unreleased).

Danny and the Juniors. "At the Hop" was number 1 in America on December 9, 1957.

**33.** *In 1957 a little-known R&B group achieved mild success with a song called "Little Darlin'." The song was also picked up by the Canadian group the Diamonds, who made it into a best-seller. A couple of years later, the group, now performing under a new name, scored its own number 1 hit with another song written by its leader. This song would become a hit twice more—in the 1960s for the Four Seasons and again in the 1970s, as recorded by Jackson Browne. The original group's third record did nothing at the time but resurfaced in 1969 as a big hit for Bill Deal and the Rhondels. What were the group's original name, the name under which it had its number 1 hit, and the names of the two songs in question?*

**34.** *In 1959 Mercury Records issued a 45 by a little-known performer featuring a song written by Chips Moman. This record went nowhere. However, both the artist and the song went on to bigger and better things. The artist, whose name was Tom Perkins but used a stage name, shortly thereafter was in the Top 5 with a rock & roll ballad classic. The Chips Moman song was unearthed a couple of years later by Gary Shelton, who also recorded under a pseudonym, and Shelton made it into a national Top 10 hit. Who were the two singers, and what were their hit songs?*

**35.** *In the early 1950s a vocal group called the Scarlets was formed in New Haven, Connecticut. By 1956 the group had changed its name. Meanwhile, its leader was drafted into the Army, where he wrote a song while on late-night guard duty. The group recorded the song during its leader's brief leave. The singer was sent to Japan before the record was released. Although it was a regional hit and never got higher than number 24 on Billboard's pop charts, today that song is one of the most requested rock & roll ballads of all time and a multi-million seller. What was the song, what was the group, and who was its leader?*

**33.** The group was called the Gladiolas when it recorded "Little Darlin'." When it changed its name to Maurice Williams and the Zodiacs, the group hit with "Stay." One of the Zodiacs' other obscurities was "May I," a beach-beat classic that was also revived and became a hit for Deal in 1969.

**34.** Perkins, who used his first and middle names, Thomas Wayne, hit big with "Tragedy" on the Fernwood label. The Chips Moman song was "This Time." Gary Shelton, better known as Troy Shondell, hit with the song in 1961.

**35.** The song is called "In the Still of the Nite." It was written, in part as a Cole Porter tribute, by Fred Parris of the Five Satins. Even after twenty-five years, the Satins' doo-wop masterpiece regularly appears as the number 1 requested oldie in radio station surveys up and down the East Coast.

**36.** When did stereophonic discs first become available to the general public? What impact did they have on rock & roll?

---

**37.** Name three artists whose names, when appearing on their record labels, were always followed by a description of the instruments they played.

---

**38.** What 1950s group included Bob Gaudio, who later went on to join the Four Seasons?

---

**39.** In September 1958 a songwriter had an idea for a Christmas song while on his way to work. He called the song "In a Village Park." He felt something was missing, however, so he made some changes (including the title) and recorded it pseudonymously as a studio "singing group." The songwriter was fairly well-known at the time, with hits such as Rosemary Clooney's "Come On-a My House," but this Christmas song was to become the biggest hit of his career. What name did the songwriter usually record under, what was the name of his studio "group" and, for extra credit, where did he get the individual names for the fictitious group members?

---

**40.** In late 1958 a young singer named Bobby Pedrick, Jr., scored a minor Top 100 hit with a song called "White Bucks and Saddle Shoes," then promptly disappeared from the charts. Many years later, the singer used his first and middle names to record some very big hits. Who was he?

36. The first stereo discs weren't really commercially produced for general consumption. After the first practical stereo cartridge and record were demonstrated at a record show in late 1957, several audiophile-oriented companies produced demonstration items in the following months. It wasn't until June 1958, though, that major record labels began offering a catalog of stereo albums to the public. Few of these records were rock & roll; since stereo was an expensive device, most releases tended to be "highbrow" music like classics and sound tracks. In 1959 stereo rock & roll discs finally became available in quantity to the public, though it was the better part of a decade before monaural discs were phased out completely.

37. Duane Eddy and His Twangy Guitar; Jerry Lee Lewis and His Pumping Piano; Boots Randolph and his Yakety Sax.

38. The Royal Teens, well-known for their 1958 hit "Short Shorts." The group's lineup later included Al Kooper.

39. Ross Bagdasarian, better known as David Seville, was the writer whose "In a Village Park" became "The Chipmunk Song," featuring Simon, Theodore, and Alvin. The three chipmunks, all of whose voices were actually done by Bagdasarian himself using altered tape speeds, were named after three Liberty Records employees, recording engineer Ted Keep and executives Simon Waronker and Al Bennett.

40. Pedrick shed his last name and became Robert John, whose chart successes include 1968's "If You Don't Want My Love," a 1972 remake of the number 3 hit "The Lion Sleeps Tonight," and the 1979 number 1 hit "Sad Eyes."

**41.** What is the relationship between "Mr. Bass Man" and the 1968 bubblegum hit "Cinnamon"?

_____

**42.** The recording career of one of rock & roll's most enduring writer/performers began when he failed to get Little Anthony and the Imperials to release one of his songs. They recorded the tune, but when it wasn't issued as a single, the songwriter put it out himself. The song jumped onto the Top 20 and started a string of hits for the songwriter, who's still making records today. Meanwhile the song chosen in its place by Little Anthony didn't do nearly as well. Who was the singer/ songwriter, and what was his song?

_____

**43.** Which 1958 rock & roll movie featured Russ Tamblyn, Mamie Van Doren, a dope bust, and a rock & roll star singing the title song from the back of a flatbed truck?

_____

**44.** Who was Dick Clark's announcer during the seminal years of American Bandstand?

_____

**45.** Singer Bill Parsons recorded several songs at a 1958 recording session. At the same session, a friend of his recorded a satire of Elvis Presley's recent Army induction called "All-American Boy" and was then drafted. While serving, Parsons's friend heard "All-American Boy" on the radio. Unfortunately, due to a record company mix-up, the song was credited to Bill Parsons; the actual singer's name was nowhere to be found on the record. Later this friend of Parsons would have dozens of hits, mostly on the country charts. Who was Parsons's friend?

41. They were both recorded by the same artist. But "Mr. Bass Man" was credited to Johnny Cymbal in 1963 and "Cinnamon" to Derek.

42. The singer/songwriter was Neil Sedaka, who brought "The Diary" to Little Anthony and the Imperials. Although the group liked the song and recorded it, its management released a different song, "So Much," to follow up "Tears on My Pillow." "So Much" flopped. The group's recording of "The Diary" can be heard on its first End album. Meanwhile Sedaka's own recording of "The Diary" launched a long string of hits for him.

43. *High School Confidential.* Jerry Lee Lewis sang the title tune.

44. Charley O'Donnell.

45. The singer on "All-American Boy" is Bobby Bare, who had several national Pop Top 40 hits ("Shame on Me," "Detroit City," "500 Miles Away from Home," and "Miller's Cave") before racking up dozens of country hits through the sixties, seventies, and eighties. Bill Parsons's voice never made the charts.

**46.** In the late 1950s a Cincinnati trio recorded "I'm Gonna Knock on Your Door," which later became a big hit for 14-year-old Eddie Hodges, and "Respectable," which made the U.S. Top 15 when recorded by the Outsiders. Neither of the original recordings, however, was successful. But the trio did come up with a gospel-oriented hit in 1959 that was later redone by countless artists. (Three other versions of the song also made the Top 100.) After a few isolated hits in the early and mid-1960s, the group finally began stringing them together, starting in 1969, when it formed its own label. Today the group is one of the best-known and most successful soul acts in the world. Who are they? What was their only fifties hit?

**47.** Harold Jenkins, so the story goes, made up his recording pseudonym by reading a map and picking out the names of two towns. His first chart record, "I Need Your Lovin'," on Mercury in 1957, made it to number 93 on the national charts. His next chart appearance came about a year later; this time he made number 1. What was his stage name, what was his number 1 hit in 1958, and what is he doing today?

**48.** Chuck Berry is obviously one of the unqualified pioneering geniuses in rock's history, and his songs have been recorded or performed by virtually every important rock band. What was his first number 1 hit?

**49.** How many times has Chuck Berry been nominated for a Grammy?

**50.** Name the odd man out in this group of early rock stars:

a. Little Richard
b. Eddie Cochran
c. Gene Vincent

d. Fats Domino
e. Elvis Presley.

46. The Isley Brothers, whose not-so-successful fifties record-ings today are looked upon by collectors as obscure gems, broke through in 1959 with "Shout." "Shout" also charted in subsequent renditions by Lulu, Joey Dee and the Starliters, and the Chambers Brothers. It was a prelude to the Isleys' own, even bigger 1962 hit, "Twist and Shout." Today the expanded group, featuring an instrumental lineup and the original singers, has about fifty pop or R&B national hits to its credit.

47. Harold Jenkins is better known as Conway Twitty, after Conway, Arkansas, and Twitty, Texas. His 1958 hit was "It's Only Make Believe." By 1962 Twitty had run out of steam as a rock & roller, so he switched record labels and became more or less exclusively a country artist. His records have been in the country & western Top 10 almost constantly since 1966.

48. "My Ding-a-Ling," released in 1972. Berry had five Top 10 hits in the fifties, including "Maybellene," "School Day," "Rock & Roll Music," "Sweet Little Sixteen" (which made number 2), and "Johnny B. Goode." But none of those hit number 1, and neither did his biggest hit of the sixties, "No Particular Place to Go," which stalled at 10.

49. None. But he received a special Grammy at the 1983 awards ceremony.

50. Elvis was the only one not to appear in the 1957 film *The Girl Can't Help It.*

51. One of Vee-Jay Records' biggest hits of 1958 was a slow vocal done by a quintet that would be very successful in the sixties. Calvin Carter, Vee-Jay's artists and repertoire (A&R) man, decided to give the singer extra credit on the record label, a move that caused so much friction in the group that the lead singer eventually went solo. The others, retaining the group name and led by an accomplished songwriter and guitar player, began to chart hit after hit starting in 1962. Who was the original lead singer, what was the group, and what was the 1958 hit?

52. In 1958 a youngster in Los Angeles who'd expected to make his career as a court reporter instead formed a singing group with his ex-high school classmates, Marshall Lieb and Annette Kleinbard. The group soon cut a national hit, using a song written by the erstwhile reporter and inspired by his father. The young writer became one of the biggest names in rock & roll in the sixties. Who was he, and what was his 1958 hit?

53. Richard Valenzuela was a high school student in California when his singing and guitar playing started winning him success. In 1958, he wrote a song for his Anglo girlfriend, whose father was keeping them apart because Valenzuela was a Mexican-American. After she cried when hearing it over the phone, he recorded it and it became his biggest success. What was this big 1958 hit, and under what name did Valenzuela record?

51. The 1958 hit was "For Your Precious Love," credited to Jerry Butler and the Impressions. Butler split from the group shortly after the hit and later had many successes, ranging from "He Will Break Your Heart" to "Only the Strong Survive." The other Impressions, headed by songwriter/guitarist Curtis Mayfield, finally struck chart gold in 1961 with "Gypsy Woman" and went on for nearly two decades.

52. He was Phil Spector, who recorded "To Know Him Is to Love Him" with his group, the Teddy Bears. Spector took the song's title from his father's tombstone. The record went to number 1 nationally. Spector's more enduring fame, however, came from his productions of the sixties, with groups such as the Crystals, the Ronettes, and the Righteous Brothers.

53. Richard Valenzuela called himself Ritchie Valens, and the song was "Donna," written for girlfriend Donna Ludwig. Valens died in the 1959 plane crash that killed Buddy Holly and the Big Bopper.

Phil Spector in 1969 with one of his bigger acts, Bill Russell.

**54.** *Tony Williams of the Platters had the same reason for not wanting to record "The Great Pretender" as the Shirelles had for not wanting to record "Will You Love Me Tomorrow." What was it?*

**55.** *In the late fifties Huey "Piano" Smith (of "Rockin' Pneumonia and the Boogie Woogie Flu" fame) recorded a song for Ace Records using the new two-track recording equipment. Because Huey already had a hit on the charts, Ace owner Johnny Vincent used one of the tracks of the tape to record another young singer's voice over the Huey Smith instrumental track. The song gave the youngster a smash hit in 1959. Who was the singer, and what was the song?*

**56.** *When John Corville, a young Texan, met an ex-disc jockey from his home state in the late fifties, the meeting led to a recording by Corville. The ex-DJ wrote and produced the song and even sang background vocals, which consisted of some rather unusual sounds. The record went on to become a number 1 million-seller. What was it, who was Corville's mentor, and what was his hit record?*

**57.** *In 1959 executives at a rhythm & blues record company decided to try letting an independent production team work with a newly re-formed group. The producers experimented with strings, tympani, and Latin rhythms, but the execs hated the resulting master tape, saying, in essence, that the record stunk, the group was off-key, and everything about it was wrong. But the more the producers listened, the better it sounded, and they finally persuaded the company to release the song as a single. It became one of the landmark records of rock & roll. Name the parties involved and the record.*

54. They believed the songs were "hillbilly."

___

55. The song was "Sea Cruise," by Frankie Ford. Vincent apparently liked that track *a lot*: When he reactivated Ace in 1971, after several years' hiatus, he kicked off with Little Shelton singing over the *same* music, though with an "updated" lead guitar part.

___

56. John Preston Corville dropped his last name for recording purposes and became Johnny Preston. The ex-disc jockey was J. P. Richardson, better known as the Big Bopper, who can be heard making the Indian sounds in the background of "Running Bear."

___

57. "There Goes My Baby" by the Drifters was produced by Leiber and Stoller with Stan Applebaum. The record execs were the ordinarily astute owners of Atlantic, Ahmet Ertegun and Jerry Wexler. For a record almost thrown away, it did quite well, making number 1 on the R&B charts and number 2 on the pop charts. Ben E. King sang lead.

**58.** What rock & roll landmark is located at 1619 Broadway in New York City?

_____

**59.** The first group to win the Grammy for Best R&B Recording (1958) was named after the horse belonging to its label owner, Gene Autry. What was the song, the group, and the horse's name?

_____

**60.** "Stranded in the Jungle" was successful for three different groups in 1956. One of these was the Gadabouts. Name the other two. What unusual characteristic did they share?

_____

**61.** In 1957 a North Carolinian using the name Johnny Dee made the national Top 40 with a song he'd written about going to the movies. Dee's song was covered by another singer, who did even better with it. Name the song and the cover artist. What other impact did Johnny Dee have on rock & roll?

_____

**62.** What is Paul Anka's only redeeming quality?

58. The Brill Building, a rock & roll landmark for having housed the most creative coterie of songwriters of the sixties—including Neil Sedaka, Ellie Greenwich and Jeff Barry, Carole King, Gerry Goffin, Bob Crewe, Phil Spector, and others.

59. With their rendition of "Tequila," the Champs beat out the competition, including Nat King Cole, George Shearing, and Perez Prado, to win the first R&B Grammy. The horse's name was Champion. (With the marginal exception of Cole, none of these nominees played R&B, establishing a Grammy tradition.)

60. The other two groups were the Cadets and the Jayhawks. Both of these groups were probably better known by other names and each used different names simultaneously. The Cadets were also known as the Jacks, who had a Top 5 R&B hit in 1955 with "Why Don't You Write Me?" The Jayhawks were better known as the Vibrations, who made "The Watusi" in 1961 and had a second hit, "Peanut Butter," that year as the Marathons.

61. The song was "Sittin' in the Balcony," which Dee recorded on the Carolina-based Colonial label. It was covered that same year by Eddie Cochran, who made his national Top 20 debut with it. Johnny Dee was actually John D. Loudermilk, who had several chart hits of his own ("Language of Love," "Road Hog") in the sixties. But Loudermilk's greatest contribution to rock & roll was as the writer of such hits as "Tobacco Road," "This Little Bird," and "Indian Reservation."

62. He wrote Buddy Holly's 1959 hit song "It Doesn't Matter Anymore."

63. Who gave his seat to the Big Bopper on the twin-engine plane that later crashed, killing the Bopper, Buddy Holly, and Ritchie Valens?

64. Who were the co-authors of "Maybe Baby," and what was their relationship?

65. Guitarist Johnny Otis once described it derisively as "shave and a haircut, two bits." What was he referring to?

66. What was Gene Vincent's first single, and what was on the B side?

67. What R&B singer, whose first big hit caused an uproar because it was based on "My Jesus Is All the World to Me," first played with a country & western band called the Florida Playboys?

68. In the spring of 1956 songwriter Mike Stoller and his wife took a cruise on the liner the **Andrea Doria**. On their return to the United States, the **Andrea Doria** was rammed by another ship, the **Stockholm**, off the North American coast. The ship quickly sank, but most passengers made it to lifeboats, were picked up by other ships, and were returned safely to New York. Stoller and his wife were among the survivors.

   Jerry Leiber rushed to the dock to meet the Stollers, bringing with him fresh clothing and important career news: A singer had just rediscovered a Leiber-Stoller song that had been an R&B hit in 1953. Who was it?

63. Waylon Jennings, who was on tour with Holly as one of the Crickets.

64. Ella Holly and Buddy Holly, who were mother and son, which suggests that not all parents hate their kids' brand of rock & roll.

65. Bo Diddley's trademark beat. Otis insisted that it was nothing special but merely an old blues rhythm that Diddley had borrowed. Part of his bitterness over Diddley's credit was that Otis had used the same beat for "Willie and the Hand Jive" in 1958 and disliked people thinking he had lifted it from Diddley. But Diddley did record that rhythm first. In *The Latin Tinge*, John Storm Roberts traces its origins to the rumba.

66. The first single by Gene Vincent and His Blue Caps was "Woman Love," released on June 2, 1956. The B side was "Be-Bop-a-Lula," which Vincent had written on a train en route to an Elvis look-alike contest. (Vincent won.) "Be-Bop-a-Lula" attracted more air play than "Woman Love," and by mid-June of 1956 it reached the Top 10, launching Vincent's career.

67. Ray Charles, whose first hit was "I Gotta Woman" in 1955.

68. It was at the dock that Stoller first heard that Elvis Presley, then the hottest record seller in the world, had recorded "Hound Dog," a hit for Willie Mae "Big Mama" Thornton in 1953. Leiber and Stoller went on to write a number of tunes especially for Presley, notably the scores of *Jailhouse Rock* and *King Creole*.

69. In 1946 a young songwriter sold his first song, "That Chick's Too Young to Fry," to a music publisher. The song was later recorded by Louis Jordan. In the fifties, though, the songwriter turned performer and had a hit with a song written by a former vice president of the United States. Who was the young songwriter?

70. One of the earliest true stereo rock & roll hits was "Twilight Time" by the Platters, which was recorded in early 1958. The single version, however, contains an error that was "fixed" for the LP, though it went uncorrected in the mono mix. What is the error?

71. What is the shortest Top 40 record ever?

72. Dick Clark was known for introducing Philadelphia's "teen idols" to the rest of the country through his TV shows "The Dick Clark Show" and "American Bandstand." One of the most successful of those Philadelphia idols actually started his career on records doing trumpet instrumentals. Who was he?

73. One of the more famous and successful singing duos of the sixties got its first hit in the fifties with a New York hit on the Big label. They called themselves Tom and Jerry. What was their hit, and what were their real names.?

74. What Los Angeles disc jockey and TV game show host had a Top 10 hit in the fall of 1959?

69. Tommy Edwards. Although primarily a songwriter, his biggest hit was in 1958 with "It's All in the Game," written by Charles Gates Dawes, a Chicago banker who had served as vice president under Calvin Coolidge.

---

70. In the first chorus on the mono version, Tony Williams sings, "Here, in the same and sweet old way . . ." when actually he should be singing ". . . in the *sweet* and *same* old way . . ." The error is corrected in the stereo version, and Williams sings the correct line in the second chorus of both versions.

---

71. "Some Kind-a Earthquake," by Duane Eddy in 1959, lasted only 1:17, barely long enough to jiggle the Richter scale.

---

72. Frankie Avalon, best known for his Top 10 hits "Venus," "Bobby Sox to Stockings," and "Why," began his recording career for the X label (an RCA subsidiary) with such tunes as "Trumpet Sorrento" and "Trumpet Tarantella."

---

73. The duo hit with "Hey, Schoolgirl." The flipside of the single, "Dancin' Wild," contained their real names: Paul Simon (Jerry) and Art Garfunkel (Tom). Both sides were written by Simon.

---

74. Wink Martindale, longtime radio and television star in L.A., hit with "Deck of Cards," an old country tune from the forties. In the late fifties, Martindale was a Memphis DJ and TV host on whose program Elvis sometimes appeared.

**75.** *Beverly Ross, co-writer of the Bill Haley hit "Dim, Dim the Lights (I Want Some Atmosphere)," was doing volunteer work at the Harlem YMCA when she met a thirteen-year-old boy with a song. She wrote an arrangement and brought it to a music publisher who was impressed enough to record the two of them singing it. The duo was called Ronald & Ruby. The publisher tried to sell the master to both Cadence and RCA, but due to some contractual complications, it took about a week to get the needed clearances. Fearing he'd be scooped, Archie Bleyer of Cadence recorded the song with one of his own groups, and the Cadence version and the Ronald & Ruby version on RCA came out about the same time. What was this song, what was the name of the Cadence group, and who had the hit version?*

**76.** *Whose New Orleans band contained the current tenor sax player of the Blasters and the current president of the American Federation of Musicians Local 47 in Los Angeles, both of whom were integral cogs in a mid-fifties hit-making machine?*

**77.** *Early in his career top New York disc jockey Dan Ingram did a jazz show using a different name. What name did he use, and what was the station on which the show appeared?*

**78.** *Hank Ballard is usually credited with having written the hit that Chubby Checker took to the top of the sixties charts, "The Twist." But the tune actually had been written back in 1953 as "What'cha Gonna Do." Who was the composer?*

75. Bleyer's group, the Chordettes, easily outdistanced the original duo on the song "Lollipop" in 1958. The RCA original edged into the national Top 40, but the Chordettes' version made number 2.

76. Fats Domino's band included saxman Lee Allen and drummer Earl Palmer.

77. During the late fifties Ingram was in the Connecticut area, where he did a jazz show for WECC in Bridgeport under the name Ray Taylor. At about the same time, he was doing Top 40 for WNHC in New Haven, Connecticut, so the name change may have been to avoid having the audience know he was on both stations. One of his fellow jocks at WNHC, incidentally, was Joel Sebastian, who later became famous at Detroit's WXYZ and Chicago's WCFL and who also worked in New York and Los Angeles.

78. Ahmet Ertegun, who intended it for the Drifters. Hank Ballard and the Midnighters had recorded "The Twist" just a few months before Checker had a minor 1960 hit with it. It was Chubby Checker, however, who popularized the dance. In fact, he took the song to number 1 again in 1962.

79. *What are the earliest releases by Elvis Presley to be recorded and released in true stereo?*

80. *What is the difference between the stereo version of the Clovers' "Love Potion No. 9" and the mono single?*

_____

81. *What is missing in the stereo version of the Coasters' "Yakety Yak"?*

79. None of Presley's songs recorded before he was discharged from the Army in 1960 have been released in true stereo. The first single done in stereo was "Stuck On You"/"Fame and Fortune," but there are rumors that some of his earlier material recorded for movies was multi-tracked. None of these have been released in stereo, though.

80. The original version, as recorded and available in stereo, has the group singing a verse at the end about "Love Potion No. 10." This verse was not included on the 45, replaced instead by a second run-through of one of the earlier verses.

81. A saxophone passage shortly after the break is not on the stereo version, although it appears on the single. The rest of the record is the same.

The Coasters.

**82.** *How much did RCA Records pay Sam Phillips for Elvis's Sun Records contract?*

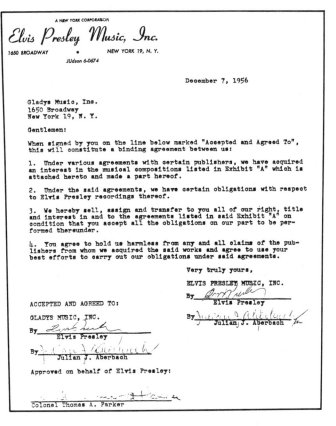

**83.** *Elvis Presley achieved a remarkable chart feat that spanned the years 1956 to 1962. No other artist has come close to matching this feat and it's not likely anyone ever will. What was it?*

**84.** *In 1947 Todd Storz, owner of KOWH, Omaha, was sitting in a coffee shop near his station's studios. Watching the customers and employees plug nickels into the jukebox, Storz made an observation that changed music history. What was it?*

82. They paid $20,000 to Phillips plus $5,000 to Elvis for back royalties. However, the deal is usually described as being made for $35,000 because Hill and Range, the Nashville music publishing company, paid Sam Phillips an additional $15,000 for rights to Phillips's song publishing company, which controlled all of Elvis's early copyrights. Presley's tie to Hill and Range was a dilemma that caused him creative problems for the next ten years.

83. From "Heartbreak Hotel" in 1956 to "Return to Sender" in 1962, every regular-issue single of Presley's placed both sides in the Top 100, and one or both sides, twenty-four straight records, reached the national Top 5.

84. Storz noticed that customers played the same favorite numbers over and over again, regardless of how often they were heard. When the shop emptied out the waitresses and countermen played the same songs even though they'd been hearing them all day. From this experience Storz developed the concept of "rotation" of hit singles in a tight pattern, which became the basis of Top 40 radio, on which all of today's pop music formats are based. Rotation is considered a key reason why radio exposure sells records.

85. *Seth Ward was a well-known radio personality in the Washington, D.C., area from the late forties through the early fifties, with his own radio show on WMAL and later on WTOP. He later recorded several hit records and after that began hawking sausage. By what name do we know Mr. Ward?*

86. *Ernest Evans started his recording career doing imitations of rock & roll singers. In 1959 he scored a hit in which he imitated several performers. When Barbara Clark, then married to Dick Clark, first met Evans, she said he looked like Fats Domino. From this remark Evans derived his stage name and went on to become the king of dance records in the sixties. Give his stage name and name his 1959 hit.*

87. *Fred Picariello was involved in the music scene very early, since his father was an orchestra leader. In the mid-fifties Fred played guitar on "Ka-Ding Dong," a hit for the G-Clefs. Three years later, in 1959, he had a big hit of his own, though not under his real name. What was Picariello's pseudonym? What was his first hit?*

88. *Ronnie Hawkins scored chart hits twice in 1959, both times with remakes of rhythm & blues songs. During the sixties, he toured using a group called the Hawks to back him up. This backup group later became famous in its own right under a different name. What was the group's more famous name? For that matter, what were Hawkins's 1959 hits, and who did the songs originally?*

89. *On the Decca album* Buddy Holly—A Rock 'n' Roll Collection *(Decca DXSE7-207), a track was mistakenly included that Buddy Holly had nothing to do with. What was the song, and who was the artist who sang on it?*

**85.** Ward is none other than Jimmy Dean, who not only brought us "Big Bad John," but also Jimmy Dean Sausage. Dean continues to work as a country music performer.

**86.** Evans recorded as Chubby Checker, an obvious takeoff on Fats Domino. His 1959 hit was "The Class." Today that hit remains a good comment on the other singers of the time, though it sounds not at all like Checker's later hits.

**87.** Fred was known as Freddy "Boom Boom" Cannon; his first hit was "Tallahassee Lassie." His mother helped him write it.

**88.** Hawkins's 1959 hits were "Mary Lou," earlier recorded by Young Jesse, and "Forty Days," a rewrite of Chuck Berry's "Thirty Days." The backup group later became known as the Band.

**89.** "Love's Made a Fool of You" is not Buddy Holly's version, but one made by the Crickets after Holly's death. It features Earl Sinks on lead vocals. The track came from the Crickets' LP *In Style*.

**90.** *Name the first rock & roll hit to use brass.*

---

**91.** *Name the Jan Berry-led duo that preceded Jan and Dean.*

Beach comedians and Beach Boy collaborators Jan and Dean.

John E. Reed

**92.** *The Farina brothers introduced rock & roll to an instrument usually associated with country music—the steel guitar. What was their big 1959 hit featuring this instrument and under what name did they record?*

51

90. "Way Down Yonder in New Orleans," by Freddy Cannon, was recorded in 1959, a full ten years before Chicago and Blood, Sweat and Tears popularized such horn sections.

91. Before there was Jan and Dean (Torrence) there was Jan and Arnie (Ginsburg). Together they got two singles to the Top 100, including "Gas Money" and "Jennie Lee," which is often miscredited to Dean. Arnie joined the Navy in 1959; that's when Dean joined Jan.

92. The Farinas used their first names, Santo and Johnny, when they hit with "Sleep Walk." They followed up with several other hits with the same general sound.

**93.** *Various hits have appeared on* Billboard's *Top 100 in more than one version. Name the artists who later had hits with these fifties originals.*

1. *"I Only Have Eyes for You," the Flamingos, 1959*
2. *"A Fool Such As I," Elvis Presley, 1959*
3. *"Only You," the Platters, 1955*
4. *"All I Have to Do Is Dream," the Everly Brothers, 1958*
5. *"Great Balls of Fire," Jerry Lee Lewis, 1958*
6. *"Do You Want to Dance," Bobby Freeman, 1958*
7. *"Lover's Question," Clyde McPhatter, 1959*
8. *"Jingle Bell Rock," Bobby Helms, 1957, 1958, 1960, 1961, and 1962*
9. *"The Big Hurt," Miss Toni Fisher, 1959*
10. *"All Shook Up," Elvis Presley, 1957*

---

**94.** *Jimmy Drake recorded several novelty songs for the Dot label in 1956. His first hit featured sounds of cars skidding and crashing. That record is now remembered as the first of a genre. Drake recorded under an unlikely name; what was it, and what was the name of his car crash extravaganza?*

---

**95.** *The concluding lyric of "Big Bad John," Jimmy Dean's 1961 hit, ". . . At the bottom of this mine lies a big, big man, Big John," was not the original ending. The first one was edited out and the above line spliced in. What did Dean originally sing?*

---

**96.** *Demos are made by songwriters as presentations to artists whom they would like to perform their work. Name three people who cut demos for Elvis Presley.*

**93.**  1. The Lettermen, 1966; Jerry Butler, 1972; Art Garfunkel, 1975
2. Bob Dylan, 1974
3. The Hilltoppers, 1955; Franck Pourcel's French Fiddles, 1959; Mr. Acker Bilk, 1963; Bobby Hatfield, 1969; Ringo Starr, 1974
4. Richard Chamberlain, 1963; Glen Campbell and Bobbie Gentry, 1970; the Nitty Gritty Dirt Band, 1975
5. Tiny Tim, 1969
6. Del Shannon, 1964; the Beach Boys, 1965; the Mamas and the Papas, 1968; Bette Midler, 1973; the Ramones, 1978
7. Ernestine Anderson, 1961; Otis Redding, 1969; Loggins and Messina, 1975
8. Bobby Rydell and Chubby Checker, 1961 and 1962
9. Del Shannon, 1966
10. Suzi Quatro, 1974

**94.** Drake called himself Nervous Norvus, and his hit was "Transfusion." The song kicked off the death rock trend: "Tell Laura I Love Her," "Last Kiss," "Leader of the Pack," etc. As Norvus, Drake also recorded other zany songs, such as "Ape Call," a takeoff on Tarzan.

**95.** Dean originally sang, "At the bottom of this mine lies a hell of a man—Big John." This version appeared on some of the earliest releases of the song but it's now quite rare. The reason for the change was undoubtedly a reaction or anticipated reaction from radio stations that frequently refused to play records containing even such mild profanity.

**96.** Brian Hyland, P. J. Proby, and Otis Blackwell.

**97.**   *Who was popularly known as "The King of the Stroll"?*

_____

**98.**   *Name the Ten Commandments of Love, according to the 1958 hit song by Harvey and the Moonglows.*

_____

**99.**   *What Olympic gold medal winner later turned rock & roll disc jockey and could be heard spinning the hits on WAAF in Chicago in the late fifties?*

_____

**100.**  *What popular New York City disc jockey had a national number 1 hit in late 1956 with a recording done in a Greenwich Village apartment?*

_____

**101.**  *Name the first group to appear on "American Bandstand."*

_____

**102.**  *Which of the following acts did not make its nationwide American TV debut on "American Bandstand"?*

    *a. Bill Haley and His Comets*
    *b. The Doors*
    *c. The Shirelles*
    *d. Public Image Ltd.*
    *e. The Jackson Five*
    *f. Buddy Holly*
    *g. Pat Benatar*
    *h. The Jefferson Airplane*
    *i. Stevie Wonder*
    *j. Otis Redding*

**97.** Chuck Willis, who was given the title by Dick Clark because the "American Bandstand" kids liked to stroll to his 1958 hit "Betty and Dupree." It was that same year that the Diamonds had a Top 10 hit with "The Stroll."

**98.** 1. Thou shall never love another.
2. Stand by me all the while.
3. Take happiness with the heartaches.
4. Go through life wearing a smile.
5. Thou shall always have faith in me in everything I say and do.
6. Love me with all your heart and soul until our life on earth is through.
7. Come to me when I am lonely.
8. Kiss me when you hold me tight.
9. Treat me sweet and gentle.
There never was a tenth.

**99.** Jesse Owens, who had won four gold medals in the 1936 Olympics, was billed as "The Fastest Moving Human Disc Jockey."

**100.** Jim Lowe, longtime New York DJ, recorded "The Green Door" in the apartment of Bob Davie, one of the writers of the song, who also played piano on the hit. The song spent three weeks at number 1 in late 1956, and altogether lasted a whopping six months on the Top 100 charts. The song was covered in the eighties by the Cramps.

**101.** The Chordettes, appearing on August 5, 1957.

**102.** Pat Benatar.

**103.** *What was the first album Phil Spector produced in true stereo?*

_____

**104.** *Jerry Lee Lewis had a 1972 Top 40 hit with a song that had been popularized by Janis Joplin—who had, in turn, lifted it from a former Rhodes scholar. What was the song?*

_____

**105.** *Robert Byrd, a singer from Los Angeles, formed a group called the Satellites, which backed him on his first solo hit in 1957. Byrd recorded under two other groups' names, both of which had national Top 100 hits. He also had several hits as a solo artist under a pseudonym. Under what name was Byrd best known, and what were his two groups? (Hint: One group was a duo.)*

_____

**106.** *Earl Nelson started his chart career with the Hollywood Flames and was the "Earl" of Bob and Earl, who had a 1964 hit with "Harlem Shuffle." In late 1965 Earl again made the national Top 50, this time under a completely new name, with a dance record. What was the hit, and under what name did Earl make his solo record?*

**103.** Spector, long known as a hater of stereo and an acknowledged mono-maniac, nevertheless produced many records in
stereo. The Ronettes' LP on Philles, for example, was all
true stereo, as was *Phil Spector's Christmas* LP (but only the
most recent reissues). The first stereo album Spector cut,
however, was the Teddy Bears' album on the Imperial label
in 1959. Unfortunately the group blended better in mono
than on separate tracks, and almost every flaw was clearly
audible. Perhaps that's why Spector's later works went to
extremes to cover any individual flaws on his recordings
with a "wall of sound."

**104.** "Me and Bobby McGee." Although "Freedom's just another
word . . ." became Joplin's epitaph, the song was written by
Kris Kristofferson.

**105.** Robert Byrd was better known as Bobby Day, who had hits
such as "Little Bitty Pretty One" (with the Satellites), "Over
and Over," and "Rockin' Robin." In late 1957 he was part of
the group the Hollywood Flames, who had a national Top 15
hit with "Buzz-Buzz-Buzz." Byrd also formed a duo called
Bob and Earl, who later hit with "Don't Ever Leave Me" and
"Harlem Shuffle."

**106.** The record was "The Duck," by Jackie Lee. Unfortunately
for Nelson, his follow-up discs tended to be rehashes of "The
Duck," such as "The Shotgun and the Duck." Even though
he was also recording at the time with Bob and Earl, further
success eluded him.

107. *In 1958 Brunswick Records released a record by a group with the unlikely name the Ding Dongs. The master was sold to Atco, a label that renamed the group and turned the disc into a national hit. The singer of the group would have a long and distinguished career as a rock & roll and pop singer for Atco and its sister label, Atlantic. Who was the singer, what was the Atco group's name, and what was the hit song?*

108. *When Elvis Presley's Top 5 smash, "One Night," was monopolizing the airwaves during the 1958 Christmas season, few people recognized it as an R&B song done years earlier by Smiley Lewis. One of the differences between the earlier version and Presley's version was in the opening lyric. Presley sang, "One night with you is what I'm now praying for..." What was the original opening line, and what famous rock & roll founding father wrote this song?*

109. *In 1958 a Detroit group had an instrumental hit with "Poor Boy," then a few years later hit again with an instrumental called "Flamingo Express." "Poor Boy" reached number 17 on the national charts, but the group would later appear on an even more successful record as the backup group to another important Detroit artist. What was the group, who was the Detroit-based singer, and on which hits did they join forces?*

110. *Which of the following groups had no Top 10 records on the national pop chart? The Flamingos; the Moonglows; the Chantels.*

**107.** The song was "Early in the Morning," with Bobby Darin singing lead. Atco called the group the Rinky-Dinks, although it was merely Darin with female backing singers. Brunswick had Buddy Holly record the same arrangement with the same women (and even the same flipside) to try to compete with Darin's version. The plan was moderately successful, as both Darin's and Holly's versions made the Top 40, but Bobby's original outsold Buddy's cover version.

**108.** The original opening line was, "One night of sin is what I'm now paying for." The song was written by Fats Domino and given to Smiley Lewis. Domino himself didn't record the song until much later. Elvis did record "One Night" with the original line—it was released on *A Legendary Performer, Vol. 4* in 1983 and can also be heard on his 1968 TV special.

**109.** The group was the Royaltones, who have had several memorable instrumentals that were regional hits, including discs such as "Our Faded Love." At the time "Our Faded Love" was issued (1964), the group was recording for the Amy/Bell/Mala labels, for which Del Shannon also recorded. The group worked with Shannon on such hits as "Keep Searchin' (We'll Follow the Sun)," "Stranger in Town," "Do You Want to Dance," and "Break Up."

**110.** None of these groups ever had a Top 10 hit, although each had many significant R&B smashes. The Flamingos came closest to the top of the pops, with "I Only Have Eyes for You," number 11 in 1959. The Chantels had two Top 15 hits, "Maybe," one of the most beautiful female R&B hits, in 1958, and 1961's "Look in My Eyes." But the closest the Moonglows ever came was number 20 with "Sincerely" in 1955. Even "The Ten Commandments of Love" (1958), by Harvey and the Moonglows, couldn't crack the Top 20.

# 3

# *When Rock Was Dead*
## (The Sixties Before The Beatles)

**111.** *Who were Benny Benjamin, Joe Messina, Earl Van Dyke, James Giddons, Robert White, and James Jamerson?*

---

**112.** *One of the biggest hits of 1960 was a ballad by a singer who once planned a career in professional baseball. While at the St. Louis Cardinals' Lynchburg, Virginia, farm team, he injured his leg sliding into second base, thus ending his baseball career. Who was he, and what was his big 1960 hit?*

111. They were the drummer, guitarist, keyboardist, precussionist, guitarist, and bassist, respectively, on almost all of Motown's greatest hits. As anonymous sessionmen and salaried employees, they often played in local bars and lounges to make ends meet. Other noteworthy Motown sessionmen included drummers Uriel Jones and Richard "Pistol" Allen, bassists Bob Babbit and Carole Kaye, percussionist Jack Ashford, and pianist Berry Gordy.

112. He was Jim Reeves, who hit with "He'll Have to Go." Reeves had great success on the country & western charts, with nine number 1 records there. Long after his death in a 1964 plane crash, his records were still making the country Top 10, as they were sparingly released over the years from material recorded before his death. Reeves was also amazingly popular in England, where he totaled more than a dozen Top 10 hits, the last one in 1972.

**113.** Fred Parris of the Five Satins wrote "In the Still of the Nite" while still in the Army. Ditto Conway Twitty and "It's Only Make Believe." Keith made "98.6" while on the lam from the Selective Service. But what was the only Top 10 hit ever recorded by a group while still on active duty?

**114.** In March 1960 Elvis Presley was discharged from the Army and promptly entered a recording studio. What was his first post-Army single, and what was unusual about its sales?

**115.** Robert Ridarelli at one time was a member of a band called Rocco and the Saints, and at nine years old was a member of the cast of the Paul Whiteman TV show in Philadelphia. Whiteman, a famed big band leader, suggested a name change for Ridarelli; what was it? For extra credit, who was the trumpet player in Rocco and the Saints?

**116.** Bill Black's Combo put eighteen different titles on the Top 100 in the sixties, including "White Silver Sands," "Don't Be Cruel," and "Blue Tango," all instrumental remakes in the combo's distinctive style. How did Bill Black first come to national fame?

**117.** Robert Velline was the lead singer for a group called the Shadows in the late fifties, when he got his professional break because of a tragedy. He later put more than three dozen titles on the best-seller charts as a solo performer. What name did he record under, and how did he get his break?

113. "Easier Said Than Done," by the Essex, whose members were still in the Marines in the summer of 1963.

---

114. Elvis's first post-Army single was "Stuck On You"/"Fame and Fortune." "Stuck on You" immediately went to number 1 on release, with more than a million *advance* sales before the record was even recorded!

---

115. Ridarelli was better known as Bobby Rydell, and he scored such early sixties hits as "We Got Love," "Wild One," "Swingin' School," and "Forget Him." His trumpet-playing pal was Frankie Avalon.

---

116. Black played bass for Elvis Presley on Presley's first Sun sides. Black and Scotty Moore were known as Scotty and Bill on the early Presley recordings. Black continued with Elvis after he moved to RCA, but left to form Bill Black's Combo in the late fifties.

---

117. Velline used the name Bobby Vee. He got his break filling in for Buddy Holly after the latter was killed in a plane crash in early 1959 in Clear Lake, Iowa. The next night in his hometown, Fargo, North Dakota, Vee joined Holly's touring edition of the Crickets onstage, filling in for Holly as the show went on regardless of the deaths. Vee later toured and recorded with original members of the Crickets.

118. *A singer who had several big hits in 1959–60 was once known as the Singing Fisherman. He attended Baylor University on a basketball scholarship but left college to fulfill a lifelong dream—to go to Alaska and work as a fisherman. He finally returned to the lower forty-eight, settled in California, and spent many years recording before he made his pop hits. Killed in a car crash in 1960, his last hit record was a tribute to his dream of years before. Who was he, and what was his last hit?*

119. *In the winter of 1960–61 a German bandleader had an international number 1 hit with an instrumental. The following year this same bandleader produced the first records recorded by a group called the Beatles. Who was the German bandleader/producer, and what was his big 1960 hit?*

120. *Probably the most successful of the Elvis imitators was a singer from Chicago. For his first hit, he recorded a song that Elvis had done on an album. From then on, the singer got his own material but continued to sound amazingly like Presley. Who was he, and what was his first hit?*

121. *Lonnie Donegan enjoyed fleeting fame in America in 1961 with his number 5 hit "Does Your Chewing Gum Lose Its Flavor (on the Bedpost Over Night)?" and then faded, only to return a full seventeen years later to produce an album noted for something other than its musical accomplishment. Name this album.*

**118.** The singer was Johnny Horton. Scarcely six weeks after "North to Alaska" entered the charts, Horton was killed as he drove through his native Texas on the way to a disc jockey convention.

**119.** He was Bert Kaempfert, and his hit was "Wonderland by Night." In 1961 he produced some songs for Polydor that featured the Beatles as backing group for pop vocalist Tony Sheridan. These sides have been endlessly reissued but remain the most banal music with which the Beatles were ever associated.

**120.** He was Ral Donner, whose first hit (with the Starfires in 1961), "Girl of My Best Friend," had been a Presley LP cut. Donner followed that hit with "You Don't Know What You've Got (Until You Lose It)," "Please Don't Go," "She's Everything (I Wanted You to Be)," and "(What a Sad Way) To Love Someone," all Presley soundalikes. In 1981 Donner did the voice-over narration (written from Elvis's point of view) for the film *This Is Elvis*.

**121.** *Putting on the Style* was recorded at the suggestion of Paul McCartney. Sidemen on the album included Elton John, Leo Sayer, Ringo Starr, Ron Wood, Rory Gallagher, and Adam Faith, who produced the set. It was released in 1978, Donegan didn't mean much in the States, but his 1956 hit, "Rock Island Line," inspired thousands of British kids, including Lennon and McCartney, to become musicians.

She mended her ways and became TV's favorite mom. No wonder her son, Ricky Nelson, was a travelin' man.

**122.** *In 1961 the song with the longest title ever to make* Billboard's *Top 100 made it to number 35. Name the song.*

**123.** *Some of the earliest recordings of the Chambers Brothers were done for the Horizon label in 1962, on which they backed up a folk singer on several singles. Who was this singer?*

**124.** *In early 1962 the fledgling Motown label scored a minor hit with a Jackie Wilson-derived song called "Jamie." Later the performer made an enormous contribution to the success of Motown in the sixties, even though he charted only four songs as a singer. Explain.*

**125.** *What R&B group had two different versions of the same song competing on the charts in 1961?*

122. "Jeremiah Peabody's Poly Unsaturated Quick Dissolving Fast Acting Pleasant Tasting Green & Purple Pills." Ray Stevens, known as perpetrator of such novelty songs as "Ahab, the Arab" and "The Streak," recorded it. Stevens went on to make a long series of country-pop hits, and in 1970 he had his own summer-replacement TV show, "Andy Williams Presents the Ray Stevens Show."

123. The Chambers Brothers backed up Hoyt Axton on an early release of "Greenback Dollar" before the Kingston Trio made it a hit, as well as a few other singles. The Chambers Brothers and Hoyt Axton were both popular club acts at the time in Los Angeles, along with then-unknown Barry McGuire, Roger McGuinn (before his days with the Byrds), and many blues singers.

124. The singer was Eddie Holland, whose contribution to Motown's success was much more related to his songwriting than to his vocal talent. Along with his brother Brian and their friend Lamont Dozier, the trio (Holland/Dozier/Holland) wrote dozens of Motown hits, such as "Baby I Need Your Loving" for the Four Tops and "Baby Love" for the Supremes. (Brian and Lamont, but not Eddie, were also the label's hottest producers.) Eddie Holland also had a minor R&B hit with "Leaving Here," recorded by a number of rock groups, including the Who.

125. Gladys Knight and the Pips, through a complicated series of contracts and agreements, ended up with the song "Every Beat of My Heart" being released on Vee-Jay "by the Pips" while the same song (though in a different recording) was issued on Fury "by Gladys Knight." The Vee-Jay version did better, making number 6; the Fury version only got to number 45.

In 1962 the Contours hit big with "Do You Love Me," which went on to become a rock & roll classic. Unfortunately, the group never even came close to matching that first success.

126. *Ron Scully started his career doing a polka show on a small-town radio station, where he was known as Polka Ron. He picked up his air name when working in Appleton, Wisconsin, at "the Happy Wapple, WAPL," when the program director named him after a lake he had just visited while on vacation. Scully, over his career, was on the air in Milwaukee, Cleveland, and Baltimore, but he's best remembered as the early-evening DJ at WLS in Chicago during the sixties. His trademarks while at WLS were a weird character who hung out on the studio windowsill, and a never-ending feud with Clark Weber, WLS's program director. Who was he, and for extra credit, who was his windowsill friend?*

127. *On the 1961 Top 40 hit "Halfway to Paradise" the singer is backed by a girl group making its first record. The girl group would record several hits of its own in the sixties, and the singer would become a star of the seventies. Who were the artists?*

126. While at WAPL, Scully was dubbed "Smiley Riley," after Lake Riley. By the time he moved to WOKY in Milwaukee, he at least got his first name back and became Ron Riley, longtime WLS and WCFL jock in Chicago. His mythical character was Bruce Lovely, who always seemed to have something bad to say about everybody. The Riley–Weber feud went on for years, even after Riley left the city. In fact Riley still periodically phones in to Clark Weber's show to exchange insults. Riley went on to become program director and then operations manager at WCAO in Baltimore, where he also does TV.

127. The singer was Tony Orlando, who later became the leader of the group Dawn, which quickly became Tony Orlando and Dawn. The girl group was the Cookies, who had hits with "Chains," "Don't Say Nothin' Bad (About My Baby)," and others. Among the members of the Cookies was singer/songwriter Carole King.

128. In 1963 a group from Raton, New Mexico, had several instrumental hits, including "Vaquero (Cowboy)" and "Quite a Party," but its career seemed to be sliding downhill. Then Norman Petty, the Clovis, New Mexico, producer who had helped develop Buddy Holly, introduced George Tomsco, Stan Lark, Eric Budd, and Doug Roberts to a singer from Texas. The singer and the group joined forces and soon had a national number 1 hit. Who was the singer, what was the group, and what was their hit?

129. One of the biggest hits of 1961 was a song based on an African folk tune, "Wimoweh." Who had this hit, what was the name of the song, and what connection did it have with the R&B group the Dukays?

130. What former Mouseketeer and star of "The Rifleman" TV series had several teen idol-style rock & roll hits during the early sixties?

131. James Ercolani was a Philadelphia boy who admired Bobby Darin's singing. In the early sixties Ercolani recorded several national hits under a pseudonym. Who was he, and what were his biggest hits?

132. How many Top 10 hits did the Ronettes have? Name them.

128. The group from Raton was the Fireballs, who also had hits with "Torquay" and "Bulldog" early in its career. The singer was Jimmy Gilmer, and as Jimmy Gilmer and the Fireballs, they struck gold in 1963 with "Sugar Shack." In the following year they charted again with a song called "Daisy Petal Pickin'." The group had another Top 10 hit in 1968 with "Bottle of Wine."

129. The Tokens had the hit. Loosely translated, *wimoweh* means "the lion is sleeping," and the Tokens turned this into "The Lion Sleeps Tonight." Shortly after the Tokens hit number 1, the Dukays recorded an answer song of sorts called "Please Help," in which they sing of running around the jungle trying to escape the lion, who is now awake and hungry. How did the lion awaken? The Dukays hit a few bars of high notes, à la the Tokens, and conclude, "Them singers? They woke him up!"

130. Johnny Crawford, one of the original Mouseketeers and co-star of TV's "The Rifleman" with Chuck Connors, hit in the early sixties with "Cindy's Birthday," "Rumors," "Proud," and others.

131. James Darren, billed as Jimmy Darren on his first release, hit with "Goodbye Cruel World" (1961), "Her Royal Majesty" and "Conscience" (both 1962), and "All" (1967), among others. Bobby Darin also used a pseudonym; he was actually Walden Robert Cassotto.

132. Despite their legendary status, the Ronettes' only Top 10 hit was "Be My Baby" (1963). "Walking in the Rain," the trio's next biggest hit, made it only to number 23.

**133.** What late fifties and early sixties R&B group from Detroit included, at various times, Wilson Pickett, Eddie Floyd, Joe Stubbs (brother of Levi Stubbs of the Four Tops), and Sir Mack Rice? What were the group's two biggest hits?

---

**134.** James Hudson had a minor hit in 1963 on a label owned by Lloyd Price. What was this hit, and what earlier success had Hudson achieved as part of a group?

---

**135.** In 1961 a band once known as the Royal Spades recorded a song called "Last Night" and followed up that hit with "Morning After." In what way was this group fundamentally important to rock & roll?

---

**136.** During the early sixties, before the Beatles arrived, rock may have "died," but soul prospered, especially in Detroit. Which was the most successful Motown act on the record charts during 1961–63, when Berry Gordy and Co. were just getting started?

---

**137.** What well-known Atlanta R&B group scored its first national hit in 1962 on the small Arlen label with a song recorded in Muscle Shoals, Alabama, at Rick Hall's Fame Studios?

133.  The group was the Falcons, who hit with "You're So Fine," recorded in a basement in 1959. After several minor hits, "I Found a Love" (with the Ohio Players—known in the sixties, more accurately, as the Ohio Untouchables—as their band) made the R&B Top 10 in 1962. Floyd and Pickett found major success as soul writers/performers. Rice wrote one of Pickett's biggest hits, "Mustang Sally."

134.  James "Pookie" Hudson hit in 1963 with "I Know I Know." Hudson had earlier been a member of the Spaniels, who made the original version of "Goodnite Sweetheart, Goodnite," as well as Top 10 R&B hits "Baby It's You," "Everyone's Laughing," and "You Painted Pictures."

135.  The original Mar-Keys (the group's name when it recorded "Last Night") contained, among others, Steven Cropper and Donald "Duck" Dunn. Cropper and Dunn did much to shape what would become known in the late sixties as "the Memphis sound" through session work at Stax Records and as part of Booker T. and the M.G.s.

136.  Surprisingly, even though the Miracles (with Smokey Robinson) were with Motown from the beginning, from 1961 to 1963, Mary Wells was the top Motown act, with three Top 10 pop and nine Top 10 R&B hits. The Miracles charted more records during this period but they didn't rank as highly.

137.  The Tams first hit was "Untie Me." Later they switched to ABC Records and hit with "What Kind of Fool (Do You Think I Am)," "Hey Girl Don't Bother Me," and others. The Tams became one of the most popular R&B bands in the southeast, a mainstay of the "beach music" sound of the Carolinas.

**138.** *Although Carole King wrote numerous pop classics for other artists during the sixties, she had only one hit during that period. What was it?*

_____

**139.** *The Ventures are the all-time bestselling rock & roll instrumental group. Name their three Top 10 singles. When did the group break up?*

_____

**140.** *One successful vocal group from the sixties got a rather slow start with its first record, "Tonight" (from* West Side Story*), which sold poorly. In early 1962 the group recorded its second single, "Dawning." This one also fared badly until its flipside started getting air play on the West Coast. The B side was soon in the national Top 5. But the group couldn't repeat its success, and its next three records flopped. When the group finally had another hit, its original lead singer, John Traynor, had been replaced by David Black. Black's singing soon made the group a fixture on the Top 40. Who was this group, and what was its flipside hit? What was John Traynor doing before he joined?*

_____

**141.** *In 1962 this singer/songwriter had minor success with two songs he had written, "Along Came Linda" and "I'll Remember Carol." Later in the sixties he teamed up with another singer/songwriter to become part of one of the most successful songwriting teams of the sixties. As singers, the duo also had several hits of their own. Who was this duo, and what were their hits?*

138. "It Might As Well Rain Until September," a number 22 hit in 1962.

---

139. "Walk—Don't Run," "Walk—Don't Run '64," and "Hawaii Five-O." They didn't break up; although they haven't made a major-label record in the eighties, they still play live concerts.

---

140. The group was Jay and the Americans, who initially featured John "Jay" Traynor on lead vocals. Traynor had previously been singing with the Mystics ("Hushabye"). Their flipside hit was "She Cried," which took several months to show up in the charts. David Black changed his name to Jay Black upon joining the group.

---

141. The singer who made the two records in 1962 was Tommy Boyce, and he joined with Bobby Hart as one of the mid-sixties' most successful songwriting teams, writing for the Monkees and several other performers. Boyce and Hart themselves hit with "Out and About," "I Wonder What She's Doing Tonite," "Goodbye Baby (I Don't Want to See You Cry)," and "Alice Long (You're Still My Favorite Girlfriend)."

142. She started out as a secretary at Motown, he as a session drummer. They each became stars in their own right after teaming up on his first Motown solo release in 1962. Name that tune and these two artists.

_____

143. In 1960 Bob Dylan picked up $50, which he really needed at the time, on a freelance harmonica job. What was the gig?

_____

144. Harold and Phil Johnson, Al Cleveland, and Arthur Crier could be heard on several early sixties hits singing background for Shirley and Lee and also on Curtis Lee's "Pretty Little Angel Eyes." What did they call themselves as a group, and what hit did they have in 1961?

_____

145. What was the first million-selling record by an all-girl group?

Martha and the Vandellas.

Marvin Gaye, a sexual healer from way back.

**142.** "Stubborn Kind of Fellow," sung by Marvin Gaye, with Martha Reeves in the background.

---

**143.** He did one song on Harry Belafonte's album *The Midnight Special* but apparently grew frustrated with Belafonte's perfectionist approach. "Over and over again," Dylan said upon quitting after just one cut. "Who needs that? The same thing again and again. That ain't singing."

---

**144.** They were known as the Halos, and in the summer of 1961 they hit with "Nag" ("You're a nag, naggety nag").

---

**145.** "Dedicated to the One I Love," by the Shirelles, 1961. The song kicked off a trend that earned the Shirelles six Top 10 discs and brought a flood of similarly styled girl groups to the charts and airwaves.

**146.** *Name two backup groups associated with Roy Orbison.*

**147.** *The career of Johnny Maestro spanned two groups and some solo singles. His biggest hit was with the Crests, "16 Candles," and on his own he made it to number 20 on* Billboard's *chart with "Model Girl" in 1961. What other group did Maestro belong to?*

**148.** *Judy Craig, Barbara Lee, Patricia Bennett, and Sylvia Peterson made up one of the most successful vocal groups of the early sixties. What names did they record under, and what other successful group produced their hits?*

**149.** *What jazz vocal group, originally called the Four Aims and better known for singing soul, toured with Billy Eckstein in support of its first* Workshop *LP (1963)?*

**150.** *Reginald Smith was an English singer who placed thirteen hits on the British charts, though in the United States he did no better than two brief chart appearances. His first was in 1960, when he made number 45 with a song under the name by which he is best known; and he also placed a record on the U.S. charts at number 47 in 1969 under a completely different name. What were his two stage names, and what were his U.S. chart records?*

146. The Teen Kings, with whom Orbison recorded "Ooby Dooby" in 1956; and the Roses, who did "Devil Doll" with Roy in 1960.

147. Brooklyn Bridge, best known for the 1969 hit "Worst That Could Happen."

148. The foursome was sometimes known as the Four Pennies ("My Block"), and also as the Chiffons ("He's So Fine," "One Fine Day," and others). Their records were produced by Bright Tunes Productions, a company owned by the Tokens.

149. The Four Tops. Workshop was Motown's jazz subsidiary, but it wasn't until after the 1963 tour that the Tops joined the parent label, began working with Holland/Dozier/Holland, and changed their name.

150. Reginald Smith was usually known as Marty Wilde, and it was as Wilde that he placed "Bad Boy" on the charts in 1960. His 1969 hit was "Abergavenny," for which he used the name Shannon.

**151.** In the early sixties a well-known R&B group recorded a song about the chances of getting ahead in the United States, but record company executives thought it sounded too odd for a black group to sing about unlimited opportunity and scrapped the song. Leiber and Stoller, producers of another (white) group, salvaged the backing track and recorded the second group doing the vocals. The song became a huge hit. What were the two groups, and what was the song?

**152.** What were the Cookies' credentials before releasing "Chains" in 1962?

**153.** This blues singer, who put nine records on the Top 100 pop charts in the early sixties, had his wife in the recording studio whispering lyrics to him as he recorded. What was his name?

**154.** In 1963 a rhythm & blues group charted with "Lonely Drifter" but could manage to get it only to number 93 on the pop charts. (Pieces of Eight would do somewhat better with the same song four years later.) The song made only a modest number 28, even on the R&B charts. The group continued this rather mediocre chart career on the Top 100 throughout the sixties, rarely rising above the 80s on the pop side. In 1972, though, the group suddenly became a crossover top seller. What was the group, and what was its most successful pop song before 1972?

**155.** Who shared lead vocals with Chubby Checker on the number 3 hit "Slow Twistin'"?

**156.** Bobby Rydell's Christmas 1961 release, "Jingle Bell Rock," recharted the following Christmas season in 1962. Who shared lead vocals with Rydell?

151. The black group was the Drifters, who also thought it was somewhat inappropriate in 1963 for blacks to be singing about becoming president. The song, "Only in America," was given to Jay and the Americans, who used the music and made it a hit. The Drifters' original version was issued many years later on a British album.

152. They were the backup singers on Little Eva's "Loco-Motion." Aldon music owner Don Kirshner was so impressed with their singing that he asked Gerry Goffin to compose material for them.

153. Jimmy Reed, whose "Baby What You Want Me to Do" and "Big Boss Man" are blues classics, recorded with Mary "Mama" Reed whispering lyrics to him just before he was to sing his lines. On some records, such as "You Don't Have to Go," Mama Reed can be heard in the released version of the song.

154. The group is the O'Jays, named for DJ Eddie O'Jay. Before they hit with "Back Stabbers" in 1972, their most successful pop song was a remake of the Benny Spellman tune "Lipstick Traces (on a Cigarette)," which made number 48.

155. Dee Dee Sharp of "Mashed Potato Time" fame. Sharp also recorded for Cameo-Parkway. She went on to marry producer Kenneth Gamble.

156. Chubby Checker. But it was Bobby Helms who hit big with "Jingle Bell Rock." Helms's version charted in 1957, 1958, 1960, 1961, and 1962.

**157.** In 1962 EMI Records had a number 1 record in England and asked Vee-Jay Records of Chicago if it wanted to release the disc in the States. Vee-Jay took the song and, as a throw-in, EMI gave Vee-Jay a five-year contract for a new group it had. What was the number 1 record, and what was the new group?

**158.** In 1962 Ginger Baker became the drummer for Alexis Korner's Blues Incorporated. Whom did he replace?

**159.** In 1962 hot rod songs became popular. The trend started in California and soon songs such as "Drag City," by Jan and Dean, and "G.T.O.," by Ronny and the Daytonas, were standard Top 40 fare. One early car song features an introduction recorded outside the writer's home late at night which had neighbors complaining about the noise. Name the song and the artist.

**160.** In 1963 Gale Garnett wrote a song called "We'll Sing in the Sunshine" for a struggling folk singer who recalled years later that he and Gale had been "going together." Upon returning to California after a road trip, however, the singer found that Gale had left, leaving only the song behind. He recorded it without commercial success. A year later Garnett recorded her own version, and it became a big hit. The folk singer later achieved success in country music, television, and motion-picture acting, as well as writing several hits for others. Today he owns his own record company and is the voice of the Busch beer commercials. Who is he?

**161.** Which of the following hits were issued in true stereo? "Sorry (I Ran All the Way Home)," by the Impalas; "Hats Off to Larry," by Del Shannon; " 'Til," by the Angels; "Tell It Like It Is," by Aaron Neville; "A Lover's Question," by Clyde McPhatter.

**157.** The number 1 hit was "I Remember You," by Frank Ifield, which also did well on this side of the Atlantic. The unknown group thrown into the deal was the Beatles, and thus the first U.S.-issued records by the Beatles were on Vee-Jay. EMI later simply walked away from the Beatles' Vee-Jay pact and Vee-Jay went bankrupt.

**158.** Charlie Watts, who went on to join the Rolling Stones. Ginger Baker joined Cream in 1966.

**159.** The opening to "409" by the Beach Boys was recorded outside the Wilson home in Hawthorne, California. Brian Wilson and co-writer Gary Usher revved up cars at the curb, which Wilson's conventional neighbors found less than amusing. If you listen to the opening of "409," you'll hear why.

**160.** Hoyt Axton, writer of such hits as "Greenback Dollar" (Kingston Trio), "Joy to the World" and "Never Been to Spain" (Three Dog Night), "The No No Song" (Ringo Starr), and "Snow Blind Friend" (Steppenwolf). His own hits include "When the Morning Comes," "Boney Fingers," and "Della and the Dealer." Axton has appeared on many television shows, as well as in motion pictures such as *The Black Stallion*. He owns Jeremiah Records, which issues his current recordings. For several years he has been heard regularly on TV admonishing us to "head for Busch beer."

**161.** They all were. The first four can be found on the stereo issues of the original albums. "A Lover's Question" was issued in stereo in the late sixties on a compilation called *History of Rhythm & Blues, Vol. 4*, on Atlantic Records.

**162.** *All of the following sixties hits made it to* Billboard's *Top 100.
Name the artists who subsequently made the Top 100 with
their versions.*

1. *"If I Were a Carpenter," Bobby Darin, 1966*
2. *"All Strung Out," Nino Tempo and April Stevens, 1966*
3. *"Good Vibrations," the Beach Boys, 1966*
4. *"I Heard It Through the Grapevine," Gladys Knight and
the Pips, 1967*
5. *"My World Is Empty Without You," the Supremes, 1966*
6. *"You've Really Got a Hold on Me," the Miracles, 1963*
7. *"Along Comes Mary," the Association, 1966*
8. *"As Tears Go By," Marianne Faithfull, 1965*
9. *"Baby I Need Your Loving," the Four Tops, 1964*
10. *"Barbara Ann," the Regents, 1961*

---

**163.** *Who plays the drums on the Shirelles' 1961 hit "Will You Love
Me Tomorrow"?*

**162.**
1. The Four Tops, 1968; Bob Seger, 1972; Leon Russell, 1974
2. John Travolta, 1977
3. Todd Rungren, 1976
4. Marvin Gaye, 1968; King Curtis, 1968; Creedence Clearwater Revival, 1976
5. Jose Feliciano, 1969
6. Gayle McCormick, 1972; Eddie Money, 1979
7. The Baja Marimba Band, 1967
8. The Rolling Stones, 1966
9. Johnny Rivers, 1967; O. C. Smith, 1970
10. The Beach Boys, 1966

Barrett Strong, the first to know that the best things in life aren't free. He recorded "Money (That's What I Want)" in 1960, but the Kingsmen had the bigger hit, in 1964.

**163.** Carole King. Writers for Don Kirshner's Aldon Music publishing company often sat in on recording sessions, helping out on a variety of tasks. Undoubtedly, King was present because she wrote "Will You Love Me Tomorrow."

**164.** *What vocal goof does Dion commit while singing "Drip Drop" (1963)?*

_____

**165.** *What early sixties instrumental smash featured the sounds of fingers tapping on a microphone and air being blown across a mike at the beginning and end of the tune?*

_____

**166.** *Name the harmonica player on Bruce Channel's "Hey! Baby" (1962).*

_____

**167.** *In 1961 Calvin Carter, head of A&R for Vee-Jay Records, walked into the mastering room of a Chicago recording studio and heard Bunky Sheppard, an independent producer, playing a tape. Carter was told the tape featured a local R&B group whose New York record company had rejected it. Carter almost immediately bought the tape for Vee-Jay. The song became a runaway best-seller, eventually going over the million mark. Name the song, the group, the lead singer, and the name under which the hit was issued.*

The high school band the Town Criers in 1963. Its rhythm guitarist, Bob Seger (at left), went on to become one of the most popular and durable singer/songwriters.

**164.** The song lyrics go, "The roof is leaking and the rain's fallin' on my head." Near the end of the song, instead of "roof," Dion starts to say "rain," then quickly corrects himself, making the word come out as "ra-oof." Considering Dion's vocal style, this was probably left in the released version because it sounds like a distinctive quirk rather than an outright mistake.

**165.** "Telstar," by the Tornadoes, which hit number 1 in late 1962, used the special effects to create a sound they hoped suggested satellites and space. "Telstar" was the first British rock song to connect in America, a good two years before Beatlemania.

**166.** Delbert McClinton, who claims he taught John Lennon to play the instrument. McClinton had his own hit, "Giving It Up for Your Love," in 1981.

**167.** The lead singer was Eugene Dixon, who recorded under the name Gene Chandler. Chandler's group, the Dukays, had had hits with "The Girl's a Devil" and "Nite Owl" on Nat Records. But for some reason, Nat passed up the chance to issue the song Carter heard Sheppard playing: "Duke of Earl."

**168.** *In a Chicago studio in 1963, Betty Everett was recording what would become her first national chart hit. After several takes the producer of the record felt something was still missing. A local vocal group was sitting in on the session, observing but not singing. During one of the playbacks the producer heard them stamping their feet through an open microphone. The song was quickly recorded again, this time including the group's foot-stomping. Name the song and the guest group whose sole contribution was made with heels and toes.*

---

**169.** *Gary Anderson started his recording career by being mistaken for a group due to his unusual nom de rock. On his second hit, the name was altered slightly to avoid the confusion, but in some circles he was still thought to be part of a promotional campaign. Identify and explain the names Anderson used.*

---

**170.** *In 1963 the Marketts scored a hit with the instrumental "Outer Limits." Name the TV show whose producer expressed offense at the song by promptly filing a lawsuit against the group, causing the song's title to be changed.*

**168.** Calvin Carter of Vee-Jay Records was recording Betty Everett with "You're No Good," a minor chart hit for Betty but a number 1 hit years later for Linda Ronstadt. The group stamping its feet on a wooden platform was the Dells, who had plenty of hits on their own, including "Stay in My Corner" and "Oh, What a Night." The foot-stomping sound also was included on Betty Everett's next record, her biggest hit, "The Shoop Shoop Song (It's in His Kiss)."

**169.** Legrand Records started Gary Anderson's career by naming him U.S. Bonds so that the phrase "Buy U.S. Bonds" could be used on his first hit, "New Orleans" (1960). (U.S. Savings Bonds were then being pushed in a widespread ad campaign using the slogan "Buy Bonds.") At first, because of the crowd noises on "New Orleans," the public thought U.S. Bonds was a group, so the name was changed to Gary (U.S.) Bonds. His biggest hit, "Quarter to Three," was a remake of an instrumental called "A Night with Daddy G" by the Church Street Five, a disc previously issued by Legrand. "Daddy G" is saxman Gene Barge, today a noted arranger/producer.

**170.** Rod Serling of "The Twilight Zone." The TV show "Outer Limits" gave the Marketts a title, but they got their music from the opening bars of "The Twilight Zone" theme, penned by series creator Rod Serling. Serling's suit must have been inspired more by competitive pique than a desire for bucks or loathing of rock, for the suit had an unusual settlement: Subsequent copies of the record were titled "Out of Limits."

171. Johnny Cymbal, most famous for his recording of "Mr. Bass Man" (with Ronnie Bright), also had a couple of hits in the late sixties under another name. Prior to "Mr. Bass Man" he had a regional hit in 1961 that predated Jaws by fourteen years but had the same general theme. What was the title of this 1961 record, what were Cymbal's pseudonymous hits, and what was the pseudonym he used?

_____

172. One of the biggest hits of 1963 was sung in a foreign language and originally appeared only on an album. When a disc jockey in the state of Washington played the cut at the end of his show one night, he was swamped with calls demanding replays. The title was unpronounceable to most Americans but roughly translated as "I Look Up When I Walk." Capitol Records changed the title of the record for its U.S. release. Name the title and artist.

_____

173. What did the Majors ("A Wonderful Dream," "She's a Trouble-maker," "A Little Bit Now [A Little Bit Later])," and the Essex ("Easier Said Than Done," "A Walkin' Miracle," "She's Got Everything") have in common?

_____

174. Bobby Goldsboro ("Honey") spent 1962–63 as a member of the band that backed one of the top balladeers of the early sixties in his live shows. Name the artist.

_____

175. Dion's version of "Ruby Baby" made it to number 2 on the charts in 1963. What group originally recorded the song?

_____

176. Brenda Reid and Herb Rooney, a soul duo recording today as Brenda and Herb, had better success in the sixties under another name. What was it?

171.   Cymbal had a minor hit with "The Water Was Red" in 1961, which told of a girl eaten by a shark. If that wasn't his low point, surely "Robinson Crusoe on Mars" in 1964 was. Cymbal went under the name Derek when he did "Cinnamon" and "Back Door Man" in the late sixties.

172.   Capitol settled on calling the song "Sukiyaki," giving the Yanks at least a fighting chance. The original title was *Ue O Mui te Aruko.* The artist was twenty-two-year-old Kyu Sakamoto from Japan. A very loose translation of the lyrics goes something like this: "I look up when I walk so the tears won't fall, remembering those happy spring days, but tonight I'm all alone./I look up when I walk, counting the stars with tearful eyes, remembering those happy summer days, but tonight I'm all alone./Happiness lies beyond the clouds, happiness lies above the sky. . . ."

173.   Members of both groups were U.S. Marines at one time or another.

174.   Roy Orbison. Goldsboro was not, however, present for the recording of Orbison's greatest hits, "Oh, Pretty Woman," "Crying," or "Only the Lonely."

175.   The Drifters, in 1956, with Johnny Moore as lead vocalist.

176.   Reid and Rooney were also the nucleus of the Exciters, best known for their lively 1963 single "Tell Him."

**177.** In 1963 this singer had a minor hit with "Baby, We've Got Love." The singer was in a series of R&B groups during the fifties and went on to become a rhythm & blues star in the sixties and seventies. Who was he, and what groups did he sing with?

**178.** One of the most lasting R&B successes of the sixties, seventies, and eighties was a singer who started out doing backup vocals for acts such as the Drifters and Garnet Mimms. Who was she?

**179.** One of Gene Pitney's earliest songwriting successes was the Crystals' "He's a Rebel," which reached number 1 in 1962. Controversy has surrounded the record, however. Although the group long denied it, the lead singer on that record was apparently not LaLa Brooks, the regular lead singer of the Crystals. Who did sing lead on the song?

**180.** This group started singing at Philadelphia's Overbrook High School in 1959. By 1961 it was recording hits for the Philly-based Cameo-Parkway record label. These included "Bristol Stomp," "You Can't Sit Down," and "Hully Gully Baby." After the group broke up, its lead singer scored a number 2 hit in 1965 as a solo act. Name the group, its lead singer, and the lead singer's 1965 hit.

177. Johnnie Taylor, who had replaced Sam Cooke in the gospel-oriented Soul Stirrers, sounded somewhat like Cooke on his 1963 hit "Baby, We've Got Love." Taylor started his secular recording career as part of the Five Echoes, a Vee-Jay vocal group that never had much chart success (though its records are now in demand with collectors). Taylor later put a string of hits on the charts under his own name, the most memorable being the 1968 million-seller "Who's Making Love" and the 1976 platinum "Disco Lady."

178. Dionne Warwick started as a backup vocalist but soon began singing solo, eventually putting more than fifty songs on the national best-seller charts after her debut in 1962 with "Don't Make Me Over."

179. Darlene Love sang lead on the hit version of "He's a Rebel." Evidently Phil Spector recorded the song in Los Angeles while the Crystals were in New York, so he just used another vocalist, since his groups were largely studio concoctions anyway. Darlene Love, one of rock's grandest voices, was a member of Bob B. Soxx and the Bluejeans (of "Zip-a-Dee-Doo-Dah" fame) as well as a solo artist with her own hits, including "Wait Til' My Bobby Gets Home," and "(Today I Met) the Boy I'm Gonna Marry," the most innocent song ever recorded.

180. The group was the Dovells, featuring the eternally nasal Len Barry as lead singer. Barry hit in 1965 with the annoying "1-2-3," among other headache inducers.

Tommy James and the Shondells with Roulette Records boss Morris Levy.

**181.** *"Hanky Panky," the 1966 hit that began the career of Tommy James and the Shondells, was actually written around 1963 and recorded by a vocal group featuring both of its songwriters. Although released on at least two different singles, the song achieved no success until the Shondells' version. Name the writers and their group.*

**182.** *On March 8, 1963, the number 40 record on the WLS (Chicago) Top 40 list seemed inconspicuous, but it was actually a landmark in rock & roll history. Why?*

**183.** *Who put the "bomp" in the "bomp ba bomp ba bomp"?*

**184.** *Who put the "ram" in the "rama lama ding dong"?*

95

181. The writers were Jeff Barry and his wife, Ellie Greenwich. Their group, the Raindrops, had hits with "What a Guy" and "The Kind of Boy You Can't Forget." Barry and Greenwich were one of the most successful songwriting teams of the sixties, with many other hits to their credit, including "Da Doo Ron Ron" and "Then He Kissed Me" for the Crystals, "Be My Baby" and "Baby, I Love You" for the Ronettes, and "Chapel of Love" for the Dixie Cups. Barry had had minimal success as an artist before meeting Greenwich in 1962, but he'd already fared well as a writer, having composed Ray Peterson's ghoulish 1960 hit, "Tell Laura I Love Her."

182. The record was "Please Please Me" by the Beatles, the first time they showed up on a U.S. Top 40 list. At that time, the Beatles' records were issued on the Vee-Jay label in the United States, and Vee-Jay was located in Chicago. The song went to number 35 the next week, then dropped off the list. Art Roberts, one of the DJs on WLS at the time, started a Beatles fan club, collecting about sixty members, as he recalls. For a station the size of WLS, this was a pitifully small reaction to what would become a national frenzy less than a year later.

183. The Marcels' bass singer did in their version of "Blue Moon," which made it to number 1 in March of 1961. But it was Barry Mann who made the question famous in his hit of the same year entitled "Who Put the Bomp (In the Bomp, Bomp, Bomp)."

184. The Edsels did, when they recorded their only Top 100 hit, "Rama Lama Ding Dong," released in 1961.

# 4

## *The Nurk Twins Meet Nanker Phelge*
### (The British Invasion)

**185.** *What group was British recording executive Dick Rowe referring to when he said that "groups with guitars are on their way out"?*

_____

**186.** *On February 9, 1964, the crime rate in America was lower than at any other time in the preceding fifty years. Why?*

_____

**187.** *If you were to pick up an old copy of the English version of the Rolling Stones'* Got Live If You Want It, *why might you be very disappointed when you got home?*

**185.** The Beatles.

---

**186.** The Beatles were on "The Ed Sullivan Show." (This statistic is puzzling, since the media apparently believe that only white people like the Beatles and that only black people commit crimes.)

---

**187.** The American and British versions of this record are completely different. First of all, the English *Got Live* is an EP. Secondly, the songs on the American version were recorded at London's Royal Albert Hall in September 1966, while the EP was recorded in March 1965, when live recording techniques were even worse than they were in 1966. One of the tracks on the EP is Stones fans chanting, "We want the Stones."

The Dave Clark Five, the Beatles' first big rivals for teenage hearts in the sixties.

**188.** *From what R&B song did the Rolling Stones take the title of* Got Live If You Want It?

_____

**189.** *Who sang lead for the Dave Clark Five?*

_____

**190.** *What well-known British director directed the Dave Clark Five's 1965 film* Having a Wild Weekend?

_____

**191.** *How much were the Beatles paid for their first appearance on "The Ed Sullivan Show"?*

_____

**192.** *Who played drums on "Back in the U.S.S.R.," one of the Beatles' finest latter-period rockers?*

188. Slim Harpo's "Got Love If You Want It." Mick Jagger also swiped many elements of Harpo's vocal style.

189. Mike Smith was the lead vocalist, well-known for his Paul McCartney-like appearance. He played the keyboards as well. Dave Clark played the drums.

190. John Boorman directed the film, a rehash of *A Hard Day's Night,* which was originally titled *Catch Us If You Can,* after the film's title song. It was his first feature. Boorman went on to direct *Point Blank, Deliverance,* and *Excalibur.*

191. $2,400. The telecast was seen by 73,000,000 people.

192. "U.S.S.R." composer Paul McCartney handled the traps on the song. According to Peter Brown and Steven Gaines *(The Love You Make,* McGraw-Hill, 1983), by the time the White Album was recorded, "the Beatles' working relationship had disintegrated to the point where the only way to get anything accomplished in the studios was for one of them to wrest control for the recording of his own composition. . . . This put Paul in control most of the time. . . ." According to the same source, Ringo contributed hardly at all to the White Album. "It was a poorly kept secret . . . that after Ringo left the studios, Paul would often dub in the drum tracks himself."

**193.** *Bonnie Jo Mason recorded "I Love You Ringo" as a minor Beatlemania hit in the sixties. What stage name did Mason later use?*

**194.** *In 1964 the Beatles released "I Want to Hold Your Hand," "Can't Buy Me Love," "She Loves You," "A Hard Day's Night," and "Do You Want to Know a Secret," among others. But they lost the Grammy for Record of the Year. Who won?*

The Beatles.

**195.** *Name the first American record on which the Beatles sang.*

**196.** *Rolling Stones guitarist Brian Jones died on July 3, 1969, in the swimming pool at his home, which was previously owned by a famous writer of children's books. Name the author and his most famous creation.*

193.  Cher. Phil Spector produced this one.

194.  Stan Getz and Astrud Gilberto for "Girl from Ipanema."

195.  "My Bonnie" was released in April 1962 by Tony Sheridan and the Beat Brothers, actually the Beatles. It was the only time that the Beatles were credited as the Beat Brothers. Other records "by Tony Sheridan and the Beat Brothers" actually featured other musicians. But the music is so mediocre that it makes little difference.

196.  The home was previously owned by A. A. Milne, the creator of Winnie the Pooh. Milne and Jones did not share similar lifestyles in other repects, however—Milne could swim.

The Rolling Stones in 1971, receiving a German gold record for *Sticky Fingers*.

**197.** *David Bowie's 1973 album* Pin-Ups *was a tribute to his favorite songs of the sixties. One song, "Sorrow," is frequently cited as having had a great impact on many British bands of the sixties. Who recorded the song originally?*

**198.** *On what Beatles song does George Harrison sing the first words of "Sorrow"?*

**199.** *Which of the following musicians did* not *record with the Beatles:*

a. *Eric Clapton*          d. *Billy Preston*
b. *Andy White*           e. *George Martin.*
c. *Klaus Voormann*

**200.** *Name seven movies in which Keith Moon appeared.*

Billy Preston.

**197.** The Merseys, who never had another hit.

**198.** "Northern Song," which appears on the *Yellow Submarine* sound track. He included the lyrics "It doesn't really matter what chords I play" because the song was copyrighted by Northern Songs, which George didn't own.

**199.** Klaus Voormann. Although he played on George's, John's, and Ringo's solo albums, he never recorded with the group. He did, however, design the cover for *Revolver*.

**200.** *Tommy, The Kids Are Alright, Monterey Pop, Sextette, That'll Be the Day, 200 Motels,* and *Woodstock.*

Ms. Keith Moon and Larry Smith of the Bonzo Dog Band on a romantic stroll.

**201.**  Who is the composer of Peter and Gordon's 1966 hit "Woman"?

Peter and Gordon.

**202.**  A member of the Beatles and a member of the Who have the same birth date. Who are they?

**203.**  What was John Lennon's middle name before he changed it to Ono?

**204.**  What is David Bowie's real name, and why did he change it?

105

201. Bernard Webb, better known as Paul McCartney. McCartney wanted to see if he could be successful without the ever-present Beatles association.

202. John Lennon and John Entwistle were both born on October 9, the latter in 1944, the former in 1940.

203. Winston; he was named for Winston Churchill. Since Churchill was a Tory politician, this ought to answer for Lennon's "working class" roots, which were frail—much frailer than those of the supposedly bourgeois Paul McCartney.

204. David Jones. He changed his name to avoid confusion with Davy Jones of the Monkees, who was also British and short.

**205.** *What was the original title of the Beatles' film* Help!?

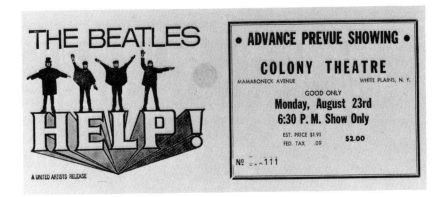

**206.** *In what year was the single "Yesterday"/"Act Naturally" released in the United Kingdom?*

_____

**207.** *What are the last names of the following singers?*

    *a. Freddie of Freddie and the Dreamers*
    *b. Gerry of Gerry and the Pacemakers*
    *c. Chad and Jeremy*
    *d. Peter and Gordon*

_____

**208.** *Who were the original Nurk Twins?*

205. *Eight Arms to Hold You*. In fact, that title still appears on the label of the highly collectible original issue of the single "Ticket to Ride"/"Yes It Is."

---

206. 1976—a full eleven years after it had made *Billboard*'s and *Cashbox*'s number 1 spot. At the time, the Beatles' British label, Parlophone, considered "Yesterday" just another *Help!* album track. When finally released in 1976, the single made the Top 10.

---

207. Garrity; Marsden; Stuart and Clyde; Asher and Waller.

---

208. Paul McCartney and his younger brother, Michael. They used the name when they performed together at childhood family functions. Paul and John Lennon also used the name for a brief period in 1960 when they did a few gigs as a duo, and later used "the Nurk twins and George" as an inside joke when referring to themselves.

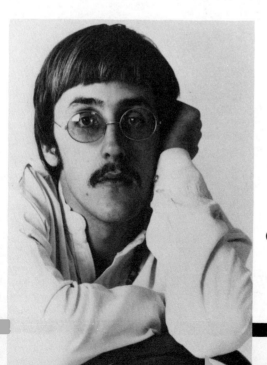

Chad, without Jeremy.

209. What was the difference between the U.S. releases and the European versions of the Beatles hits "I Want to Hold Your Hand," "I Feel Fine," and "She's a Woman"?

210. On March 27, 1964, Radio Caroline, Britain's first pirate radio station, began broadcasting from a ship based in the English Channel, giving U.K. youth their first twenty-four-hour pop music station and England its first full exposure to commercial broadcasting. What other rock-related event took place that day?

211. The Beatles recorded "I Saw Her Standing There" in 1964. Ten years later, John Lennon recorded the song again as a duet with a major rock artist on the B side of a hit single. Name the A side.

212. The Kinks' first single, recorded in the early sixties, was the same song that Paul McCartney first sang in public. Name it.

213. In how many languages did the Beatles record?

214. What is the title of the book Marc Bolan wrote?

**209.** Capitol Records added reverb to the U.S. issues of these and several other Beatles hits in an apparent effort to enhance the cuts in a way that would make them more managable for the trained American AM radio listener. That's good ol' American know-how, we guess.

**210.** The first mods-vs.-rockers riot took place at the seaside resort town Clacton-on-Sea.

**211.** "Philadelphia Freedom," by Elton John. John and Elton had recorded the live version of "I Saw Her Standing There" at a Madison Square Garden concert on Thanksgiving 1974. They also sang "Whatever Gets You Thru the Night" and "Lucy in the Sky with Diamonds" that night, and these were finally released after Lennon's death.

**212.** "Long Tall Sally." Paul was twelve when he sang the song at a summer holiday camp. The Kinks didn't have any luck with it either.

**213.** Four: English; German ("I Want to Hold Your Hand" and "She Loves You"); Italian (side 2 of *Abbey Road*—"*Cuando mon amore . . .*"); and French ("Michelle"). Five if you count the gibberish (goo-goo-ga-joob) in "I Am the Walrus."

**214.** *The Warlock of Love.* A sixty-three-page collection of Bolan's poetry, the tome was released in 1969 and, as a result of the then-current T. Rexmania, it sold 40,000 copies, making it Britain's top-selling book of poetry.

215. Name five former Rolling Stones.

_____

216. What is the significance of the Rolling Stones' song "2120 South Michigan Avenue"?

_____

217. What was the first rock album not to list song titles on its cover?

_____

218. Which of these Beatles hits have been issued in true stereo?

a. "I Want to Hold Your Hand"
b. "She Loves You"
c. "Love Me Do"
d. "Ticket to Ride"
e. "She's a Woman"
f. "Baby You're a Rich Man"

215. Ian Stewart, Dick Taylor, Mick Taylor, Brian Jones, and Billy Preston.

216. It was the Chicago address of Chess Records.

217. *The Who Sell Out.* The album was controversial among retailers because of this, although today it is regarded as an example of classic LP graphics.

218. "She Loves You" and "Love Me Do" have never been issued anywhere in true stereo. After more than fifteen years of being unavailable in stereo, "I Want to Hold Your Hand" and "Ticket to Ride" were finally issued in the United States in true stereo in the eighties. "She's a Woman" is available in true stereo only on an Australian album and an English EP set. "Baby You're a Rich Man" has been issued in stereo on certain European versions of *Magical Mystery Tour*, but it remains elusive in stereo in the States.

Roger Daltrey, well-known mime.

**219.** *Three unrelated Americans became top British teen idols in the mid-sixties. Name the group they belonged to.*

_____

**220.** *Two members of the Small Faces went on to bigger success in groups they joined after the Faces split up. Who were they, and what bands did they join?*

_____

**221.** *Name eleven bands featuring ex-members of the Yardbirds.*

_____

**222.** *Name the three experimental LPs made by John Lennon and Yoko Ono in 1968–69.*

_____

**223.** *Name four of Manfred Mann's lead singers.*

_____

**224.** *Match the performers with their British record label.*

a. The Move
b. The Troggs
c. The Who
d. Cream
e. The Beatles
f. The Kinks
g. The Rolling Stones
h. The Yardbirds
i. The Small Faces
j. The Mindbenders

1. Pye
2. Reaction
3. Decca
4. Columbia
5. Immediate
6. Fontana
7. Track
8. Regal Zonophone
9. Page One
10. Parlophone

219. The Walker Brothers, who bore a distinct vocal resemblance to another group of non-brothers, the Righteous Brothers. The Walker Brothers' real names were Gary Leeds, Scott Engel, and John Maus. They placed two tunes in the U.S. Top 20, "Make It Easy on Yourself" (1965) and "The Sun Ain't Gonna Shine (Anymore)" (1966).

220. Singer Steve Marriott broke up the Small Faces and joined Humble Pie. Kenney Jones later joined the Who. Ron Wood joined the Rolling Stones, but he was in the Faces after they were no longer Small.

221. Renaissance (Keith Relf and Jim McCarty); Cream (Eric Clapton); Led Zeppelin (Jimmy Page); Blind Faith (Eric Clapton); Derek and the Dominoes (Eric Clapton); the Jeff Beck Group (Beck); Beck, Bogert and Appice (Beck); Delaney and Bonnie and Friends (Eric Clapton); John Mayall's Bluesbreakers (Eric Clapton); Illusion (Jim McCarty); and the Plastic Ono Band (Eric Clapton).

222. *Unfinished Music Vol. #1—Two Virgins, Unfinished Music Vol. #2—Life with the Lions,* and *The Wedding Album.*

223. Mike D'Abo, Paul Jones, Chris Thompson, and Mick Rogers. Manfred Mann himself did some leads in the late seventies with his Earth Band.

224. a—8; b—9; c—7; d—2; e—10; f—1; g—3; h—4; i—5; j—6.

**225.**   *Name two hits on which Jeff Beck is an uncredited guitarist.*

_____

**226.**   *Mickie Most is the owner of one of the world's most successful independent labels, RAK. He is also a well-known producer. Name twelve of his production clients who've had U.K. or American hits.*

_____

**227.**   *In 1966 Paul McCartney made a cameo appearance on a flower-power hit. Name the song.*

_____

**228.**   *Name five sixties hits written by 10cc's Graham Gouldman. Of what British Invasion group was Gouldman a member?*

_____

**229.**   *What album-cover artist was a member of Manfred Mann in one of its late sixties incarnations and also replaced Jack Bruce when he left Cream?*

The original Manfred
Mann lineup.

225. "Hurdy Gurdy Man," by Donovan; and "Superstition," by Stevie Wonder.

226. The Yardbirds, Herman's Hermits, Lulu, Donovan, the Jeff Beck Group, the Animals, Suzi Quatro, Nashville Teens, Hot Chocolate, Mud, Chris Spedding, C.C.S., and Kim Wilde.

227. "Mellow Yellow," by Donovan.

228. The Yardbirds' "Heart Full of Soul" and "For Your Love," Herman's Hermits' "Listen People" and "No Milk Today," and the Hollies' "Bus Stop." Gouldman was a member of the Mindbenders, who had hits with "A Groovy Kind of Love" and "Game of Love."

229. Klaus Voormann, the Beatles' pal who designed the *Revolver* cover.

**230.** *Who played harmonica on Millie Small's 1964 ska hit, "My Boy Lollipop"?*

---

**231.** *The Beatles covered Buddy Holly's "Words of Love" and Chuck Berry's "Roll Over Beethoven." Whose song was "Devil in Her Heart"?*

---

**232.** *The Tremeloes' hit "Silence Is Golden" was originally the B side of a single by what American group?*

---

**233.** *Name two hits written by Cat Stevens for performers other than himself.*

---

**234.** *What do TV producers and rock band managers Vicki Wickham and Simon Napier-Bell have in common with Italian film score composer Pino Donnagio?*

The Animals with actor Cyril Ritchard.

**230.** Rod Stewart.

**231.** The Donays, a Motown act that never charted, had recorded the song in 1962.

**232.** The Four Seasons.

**233.** "Here Comes My Baby," for the Tremeloes; and "Wild World," for Jimmy Cliff.

**234.** Wickham (LaBelle, Nona Hendryx) and Napier-Bell (Yardbirds, Marc Bolan) wrote the English lyrics to Dusty Springfield's 1966 hit "You Don't Have to Say You Love Me," for which Donnagio wrote the melody.

235. *Name three groups that have been alleged to secretly be the Beatles.*

_____

236. *Name five performers produced or discovered by Pete Townshend.*

_____

237. *True or false: Eric Clapton was a member of each of the following:*

    a. *The Yardbirds*
    b. *Powerhouse*
    c. *Delaney and Bonnie and Friends*
    d. *The Masked Marauders*
    e. *John Mayall's Bluesbreakers*
    f. *Cream*

_____

238. *The Beatles recorded two show tunes. One was a song that had been composed by Meredith Wilson for* The Music Man; *the other was the title song from a Broadway hit. Name the songs.*

_____

239. *The Rolling Stones recorded only one Lennon-McCartney song. Which one?*

119

Andy Gibb just wants to be Wendy Williams's everything.

235. When the Bee Gees first released "The New York Mining Disaster 1941" in 1967, many people thought that the initials *B.G.* stood for "Beatles Group." Similarly, many people assumed that "Lies," by the Knickerbockers in 1966, was too much of a dead ringer to be anyone but the Fab Four. And Klaatu, a seventies Canadian band, intentionally hyped their (theoretical) resemblance to the Beatles.

236. The Crazy World of Arthur Brown, Speedy Keen, Ronnie Lane, Simon Townshend, and the Skids.

237. Either *c* or *d* is false, depending on whom you ask.

238. "Till There Was You" and "A Taste of Honey."

239. "I Wanna Be Your Man." It was the Stones' second single but their first to make the British Top 20. It was released in December 1963 and appears on their first U.S. album, *The Rolling Stones—England's Newest Hit Makers* (1964).

**240.** *In 1964 the Beatles played a concert in Kansas City. After the show, the sheets and pillowcases on which they slept were sold for $1,150 to Chicago radio station WBKB. The sheets were cut into one-inch squares, six thousand of which were sold for a dollar apiece. What happened to the pillowcases?*

**241.** *Name two countries in which John Lennon's music is banned.*

**242.** *How long does the final note of "A Day in the Life" at the end of* Sgt. Pepper's Lonely Hearts Club Band *last?*

**243.** *In 1964 Vance and the Avengers released a U.K. cover version of the Beatles' "I'll Cry Instead," which became a notable flop, earning the band ten shillings in royalties. The drummer, who ultimately became the band's lead singer, went on to become one of the most well-known and successful interpreters of the Beatles' music. Who was he?*

**244.** *What was unusual about the first three Troggs songs to make the Top 100?*

Such wild things—the Troggs.

**240.** They are in a bank vault, according to Peter Brown and Steven Gaines, who claim that the pillowcases have appreciated "more than the price of gold."

**241.** Iran, which bans all rock music; and South Africa, which has refused all sales and airplay of Lennon-connected works since his "bigger than Jesus" statement of 1966. This ban also applied to the other Beatles until it was lifted from the works of Paul, George, and Ringo in 1970.

**242.** Forty-five seconds. The note was played by a forty-two-piece orchestra, and in order to catch every last bit of the sound, the mikes were turned up so high that the Abbey Road Studio air conditioners can be heard in the background. (Bonus question for owners of manual turntables: Have you had the patience to wait for the whole thing at any time during the past ten years?)

**243.** Joe Cocker, who had taken a leave of absence from his job at a pipe-fitting shop to record. Cocker returned to his job for several months before venturing into show business again.

**244.** All three were available as singles on both the Atco and the Fontana labels, a very rare situation indeed. In fact, the group's first two hits, "Wild Thing" and "With a Girl Like You," were flipsides on Atco 6415, so if you happened to pick up the Atco "Wild Thing," for instance, you bought the Troggs' first two hits.

**245.**  *How would rock history have changed if Cass and the Casanovas had been a little bit more reliable?*

_____

**246.**  *Who were the Ladders?*

_____

**247.**  *On John Lennon's 1975 album* Rock 'n' Roll, *he sang two Chuck Berry compositions. Why?*

_____

**248.**  *Name the five men who played guitar with the Yardbirds.*

**245.** The Beatles might never have gone to Hamburg. Cass and Co. were booked to play the Indra Club in Hamburg in August of 1960 but canceled. The Beatles' then-promoter and sometime agent Alan Williams got them to fill in, and thus began those infamous nights of pill popping and wearing toilet seats around necks.

**246.** In the early seventies, right after the Beatles' breakup, John, George, and Ringo toyed with the idea of starting a new band with Klaus Voormann on bass. That band was to have been called the Ladders.

**247.** Presumably because he liked them. But also because he had been sued by Big Seven Music for copyright infringement. As the opening lines of "Come Together," Lennon had used a fragment from Berry's "You Can't Catch Me," which Big Seven controlled. Big Seven sued, and rather than fight it out in court, John agreed to perform two Big Seven songs on the album. These turned out to be "Sweet Sixteen" and—of all things—"You Can't Catch Me." The settlement led to another suit when Big Seven's sister company, Adam VIII, issued the *Rock 'n' Roll* tapes on its own label.

**248.** Anthony "Top" Topham, who was the band's guitarist in 1963, when the band was still called the Metropolis Blues Quartet, was one. He was replaced later that year by Eric Clapton, another. Also: Chris Dreja, who played rhythm guitar; Jeff Beck; and Jimmy Page.

**249.** When did the Beatles make their first appearance on American TV?

_____

**250.** Cream's "Badge" was one of those songs that sent listeners scurrying to discover hidden meanings or mysterious revelations. Where does the title come from?

_____

**251.** Why did John Lennon ask Paul McCartney to join the Quarrymen, the skiffle band that he formed in the mid-fifties?

_____

**252.** Paul McCartney has written numerous love songs for his wife, Linda. But he's not the only one to write of her charms. What other song was inspired by Mrs. McCartney?

_____

**253.** Alan Price's keyboard playing was one of the highlights of the early Animals' records, particularly on "House of the Rising Sun," where the organ work transformed the old blues standard. But Price left the Animals in 1965, right after the success of "Rising Sun," and plays on none of the band's other hits. Why did he leave the band?

249. Although "The Ed Sullivan Show" on February 9, 1964, was the Beatles' first *live* performance on American TV, their first appearance was on Jack Paar's show on January 3, 1964. He showed a tape of a November 1963 English TV program that had the Beatles singing "She Loves You."

250. "Badge" was a misreading on Eric Clapton's part. He co-wrote the song with George Harrison, and while looking over George's handwritten lyric sheet, confused "bridge" for "badge." Their amusement and confusion gave the song its enigmatic title. Harrison is billed as "L'Angelo Misterioso" on the track.

251. He was impressed that Paul not only knew how to tune a guitar but had also memorized the words to "Be-Bop-a-Lula."

252. The 1947 hit song "Linda," written by Jack Lawrence. Linda's father, Lee Eastman, an attorney, suggested to Lawrence that he write the song and publish it through an Eastman-controlled company instead of paying Eastman his legal fees. Paul McCartney now owns the song and the entire Jack Lawrence catalog.

253. The success of "House of the Rising Sun," particularly in America, was responsible for Price's departure. Price had a terrible fear of flying, and since "Rising Sun" necessitated touring, Price decided to leave the band rather than brave the harrowing trans-Atlantic trips.

254.  *Name the only American group to be signed by Brian Epstein.*

255.  *What British group placed two different songs with the same main title on the Top 100, one in 1964 and the other in 1967?*

256.  *What did LSD do for Paul McCartney?*

WABC New York DJ "Cousin" Bruce Morrow presents the WABC All-American Award to Paul McCartney.

257.  *Which of these Rolling Stones hits have been released in true stereo in the United States: "(I Can't Get No) Satisfaction"; "19th Nervous Breakdown"; "Not Fade Away"; "It's All Over Now"; "Heart of Stone"?*

254. Cyrkle, whose biggest hit, "Red Rubber Ball," was written by Paul Simon. John Lennon named the band, which opened for the Beatles on their last American tour.

255. The Dave Clark Five charted two completely different songs with the title "Everybody Knows." The first was subtitled "(I Still Love You)," but they're still confused with one another.

256. According to what Paul told *Life* magazine in 1967, it made him "a better, more honest, more tolerant member of society."

257. None have been released in true stereo in the United States. Both "Satisfaction" and "19th Nervous Breakdown" were recorded in true stereo, and rough mixes do exist, but the songs have yet to be issued in stereo anywhere in the world. "Not Fade Away" has not been issued in stereo anywhere in the world and was possibly recorded only in mono. Both "It's All Over Now" and "Heart of Stone" have been issued in true stereo on albums in the United Kingdom and elsewhere.

258.  *In their early years the Rolling Stones recorded such songs as "Now I've Got a Witness," "2120 South Michigan Avenue," "I'm All Right," "Play with Fire," and "The Under Assistant West Coast Promotion Man." All were composed by Nanker Phelge. Who was Nanker Phelge?*

_____

259.  *After the Beatles split up, Ringo had a number of hit songs, including "It Don't Come Easy" and "Back Off Boogaloo." To what does the latter song refer?*

_____

260.  *Who was the only black "Fifth Beatle"?*

_____

261.  *What is odd about the stereo format of the Beatles' "I Am the Walrus"?*

**258.** Nanker Phelge was a songwriting pseudonym for Mick Jagger and Keith Richards.

---

**259.** Paul McCartney, then suing to dissolve the Beatles' partnership. "Boogaloo" was one of Paul's code names during the Beatles' tours. The 1972 song fits in with several other bitter songs recorded by the other members of the group, such as George's "Sue Me Sue You Blues," John's "How Do You Sleep?" and Paul's "Too Many People." Ironically, Ringo made not only the biggest hit of any of these, but also the only attempt at reconciliation, with "Early 1970," the B side of "It Don't Come Easy."

---

**260.** Billy Preston, who played on "Get Back."

---

**261.** About halfway through the song, "I Am the Walrus" switches from true stereo to rechanneled stereo. EMI recently noted that, while it has the necessary tapes to mix a version of the song that's true stereo all the way through, it doesn't plan to do so.

# 5
# *The Kids Are All Wrecked*
## (The Sixties—1964 And Onwards)

262. This New York–based singer made four national Top 20 records, but none were released under his own name. He made the first in 1964 as part of a group, and he made the other three in 1969 as the studio voice of two other groups. Name him, his four hits, and the three groups.

263. What luckless group had five different songs on the Billboard "Bubbling Under" charts (numbers 101–130) yet never placed a record on the Top 100?

**262.** Ron Dante had his first hit as lead vocalist of the Detergents, whose Shangri-Las parody, "Leader of the Laundromat," made number 19 in 1965. Dante then became the voice of the Archies, who hit with "Sugar, Sugar" (number 1) and "Jingle Jangle" (number 10) in 1970. At the same time, he was the voice of the Cuff Links, who hit number 9 with "Tracy."

---

**263.** The Robbs, whose five near-misses during 1969 and 1970 included the Chicago hits "Race with the Wind," "Rapid Transit," "Movin'," "Last of the Wine," and "I'll Never Get Enough." To make things worse, the group changed its name to Cherokee and had *another* song, "Girl I've Got News for You" (1971), place on the "Bubbling Under" charts without ever cracking the Top 100.

**264.** Match the performer with the hit.

| | | | |
|---|---|---|---|
| a. | Jimmy Soul | 1. | "A Hundred Pounds of Clay" |
| b. | Nick Gilder | 2. | "Girl Watcher" |
| c. | The Wailers | 3. | "California Sun" |
| d. | Lipps, Inc. | 4. | "No Matter What Shape |
| e. | The Olympics | | (Your Stomach's In)" |
| f. | The O'kaysions | 5. | "The Night Chicago Died" |
| g. | Andrew Gold | 6. | "If You Wanna Be Happy" |
| h. | The Dramatics | 7. | "Hot Child in the City" |
| i. | The Rivieras | 8. | "Come and Get Your Love" |
| j. | The T-Bones | 9. | "Whatcha See Is Whatcha Get" |
| k. | Gene McDaniels | 10. | "Lonely Boy" |
| l. | Redbone | 11. | "Western Movies" |
| m. | Paper Lace | 12. | "Tall Cool One" |
| n. | Big Maybelle | 13. | "Funkytown" |
| | | 14. | "96 Tears" |

**265.** Phil Spector has appeared in only one film. What was it, and which role did he play?

**266.** Peter (Asher) and Gordon (Waller) had a number 1 hit in 1964 with "A World without Love." Who wrote the song? (That's the easy part.) Why?

**267.** In 1967 the Lewis and Clarke Expedition placed a record at number 64 on the national Top 100. Both "Lewis" and "Clarke" would later have hits under their own names. Name them and the Lewis and Clarke Expedition hit. On what sixties soundtrack can they be heard using their alleged first names as a duet?

264. a—6; b—7; c—12; d—13; e—11; f—2; g—10; h—9; i—3; j—4; k—1; l—8; m—5; n—14.

---

265. *Easy Rider* (1969); he had a nonspeaking part as a coke pusher. Spector also helped bankroll the film. He also is seen in a shot or two in *The T.A.M.I. Show*, but that was a kinescope, not a film.

---

266. Paul McCartney wrote it for Asher's sister, Jane, whom he was dating at the time. (Bobby Rydell also had a minor hit with the song that year.)

---

267. Travis Lewis and Boomer Clarke were two of the five members of the Lewis and Clarke Expedition, which hit with "I Feel Good (I Feel Bad)" in 1967. About the same time, as Boomer and Travis, they could be heard doing "Fowl Owl" on the sound track to *In the Heat of the Night*. Boomer was Owen Castleman, who as Boomer Castleman had the bizarre hit "Judy Mae" in 1975. Travis Lewis is much better known as Michael Murphey, who hit with "Wildfire," "Geronimo's Cadillac," "What's Forever For," and others in the seventies and eighties.

268.   On April Fools' Day 1964, New York's WABC disc jockey Dan Ingram was the victim of an elaborate prank set up by other personnel at the station. This prank has become well-known in the radio business due to widely circulated air-check tapes. What was it?

269.   Many of the Four Seasons' hits weren't released in stereo on their original albums. Two of these songs, "Dawn (Go Away)" (1964) and "Let's Hang On" (1965), eventually appeared in true stereo on the compilation Edizione d'Oro, a double-album set. The stereo versions, however, differ from the 45 versions during parts of the songs. What's the difference? What other song is in stereo on this LP for the first time anywhere?

270.   Which St. Louis choir director, who had been singing since age five at her father's church, was discovered by Little Milton, who requested that she be his band's piano player?

271.   Why did Gram Parsons leave the Byrds in 1968?

272.   Like any other hit factory, Motown often followed up hit records with soundalike songs. Which 1965 Four Tops follow-up to a number 1 song was the most blatant example of this?

**268.** That day Ingram started his show as usual but within minutes was taken off the air by station engineers. Ingram thought he was broadcasting, but the WABC audience actually heard Bob Dayton doing an alternate show from a second studio. Meanwhile some of the advertising copy to be read "live" by Ingram was changed to include off-color material. It took Ingram about twenty minutes to get the gag, and he finally burst into the auxiliary studio where Dayton was on the air. A few minutes after Ingram went back on the air, though, the station engineers pulled the switch a second time, this time substituting Sammy Kaye as the disc jockey. Ingram caught this one almost immediately.

**269.** Evidently the slow beginnings of both "Dawn" and "Let's Hang On" were added after the songs were recorded. Neither stereo version has the 45 intro, although the rest of each song is identical. Also on the LP is "Rag Doll" in stereo; that cut has not appeared elsewhere in that format.

**270.** Fontella Bass, who later recorded "Rescue Me" (1965) on her own.

**271.** He refused to take part in a tour of South Africa because of that nation's apartheid (racial segregation) policies. In this respect, Parsons was far ahead of his time, since the United Nations-sponsored boycott of South Africa didn't take hold of the show biz community until the mid-1980s.

**272.** "It's the Same Old Song" came right on the heels of the number 1 hit "I Can't Help Myself," and got to number 5 on the pop charts.

**273.** In what year did albums first outsell 45s?

_____

**274.** In his early twenties, Jimmy Page, because of his delicate health, refused to join any band with which he'd have to tour. Instead Page became one of London's most prolific session musicians. Which of the following artists did Page not record with?

a. Them
b. The Who
c. Burt Bacharach
d. The Everly Brothers
e. The Kinks
f. Tom Jones
g. Herman's Hermits
h. Brenda Lee
i. Shirley Bassey.

_____

**275.** What do the Bellamy Brothers and Percy Sledge have in common?

_____

**276.** Booker T. and the M.G.s served up "Red Beans and Rice" and Freddy McCoy offered "Peas 'n' Rice." Who used rice to concoct a heavy-metal dessert?

273. 1968. This portended a massive change in record business profits, for albums make much more money per unit than singles. It also indicated the massive change in content created by the Beatles and acid rock. In this respect, 1983 may have been a similar watershed, since it was that year that cassettes first outsold discs.

274. Shirley Bassey.

275. Not a helluva lot, but Howard Bellamy did play organ in Sledge's band in the mid-sixties.

276. Jeff Beck had "Rice Pudding" on the *Beck-Ola* menu.

Percy Sledge outside the Phil Walden offices in 1967, before they became Jimmy Carter's campaign headquarters.

**277.** *In the sixties this disc jockey had one of the most bizarre rock & roll shows ever, including hundreds of prerecorded voice and sound inserts that were dropped into the show at virtually any time. During his stay in Cleveland he once did a cowboy scene in which two cowboy voices were heard to say something along the lines of, "This town ain't big enough for both of us." "You're right. At the count of three, let's draw and fire." "One, two, three." At this point, there followed three solid minutes of war sounds (cannons, machine guns, rockets, etc.) taken from a World War II sound-effects record. At the end of this, one of the cowboy voices came back and said, "Ha, ha. You missed me!" This DJ achieved wider fame in the late sixties with his shows in Chicago. He was one of the first disc jockeys in the country to have a weekly show featuring the progressive rock "underground" music. Who was he, and what was the name of his underground rock show?*

**278.** *Match the producers with the record labels they started.*

| | |
|---|---|
| a. Nicky Chinn and Mike Chapman | 1. Planet |
| b. Jerry Leiber and Mike Stoller | 2. Philles |
| c. Sam Phillips | 3. Phillips International |
| d. Phil Spector and Lester Sill | 4. RAK |
| e. Richard Perry | 5. Immediate |
| f. Gamble and Huff | 6. Fame |
| g. Holland/Dozier/Holland | 7. Red Bird |
| h. Rick Hall | 8. Invictus/Hot Wax |
| i. Mickey Most | 9. Dreamland |
| j. Andrew Oldham | 10. Sun |

277.   Ron Britain, who's still on the air with a syndicated satellite
       radio show. Britain's current style is much more conven-
       tional than that of his shows on WCFL (Chicago) in the mid-
       to-late sixties, where virtually anything went. His under-
       ground show, "Subterranean Circus," ironically, featured
       far fewer drop-ins or other bizarre features, simply because
       Britain did not want his listeners to think he was making
       fun of the music.

---

278.   a—9; b—7; c—10; d—2; e—1; f—3; g—8; h—6; i—4; j—5.

**279.** *Name the lead singer in each of these groups.*

a. Harold Melvin and the Bluenotes
b. Billy Ward and His Dominoes
c. Paul Revere and the Raiders
d. The Spencer Davis Group
e. Manfred Mann's Earth Band
f. The Jeff Beck Group

_____

**280.** *Name two non-Beach Boys hits on which that group appears.*

_____

**281.** *What significant rock & roll event took place in New York City on April 19, 1965?*

279. a. Teddy Pendergrass
b. Jackie Wilson (Earlier, when the group was called the Dominoes, Clyde McPhatter was its lead singer.)
c. Mark Lindsay
d. Steve Winwood
e. Chris Thompson
f. Rod Stewart

---

280. "Wishing You Were Here" by Chicago (1974) and "Rock and Roll Lullaby" by B. J. Thomas (1972).

---

281. On that day rock station WINS switched from pop music to all news. This signaled a national trend away from AM music programming which has gained momentum over the years—unfortunately for fans of Top 40 rock & roll.

WINS DJs Murray the K (left) and Johnny Holliday (right) with Julie Ross and Frankie Avalon in 1964.

**282.** *This nationally famous disc jockey has worked at stations in Los Angeles, Chicago, and Buffalo. He had one of the first syndicated rock & roll shows in the mid-sixties, and his shows were noted for zaniness, strangely flavored pizzas, and knock-knock jokes. Who is he? What's his nickname? For extra credit, what was unusual about his appearance when he did high school hops early in his career?*

_____

**283.** *The novelty record "Report to the Nation," by Winkly and Nutly, was actually done by two West Coast disc jockeys. Who were they?*

_____

**284.** *What inspired the name Buffalo Springfield?*

_____

**285.** *Who was the drummer listed as "You Know Who" on Jeff Beck's* Truth *album (1968)?*

282. Dick Biondi, also known as "The Wild Itralian." Early in his career, he used to show up at hops with his hair and beard dyed in the school colors. His "Pizza Song," while at WLS in Chicago, predated Tom Glazer's hit "On Top of Spaghetti" by more than a year; the songs were very similar. His use of the phrase "There's a fungus among us," taken from the old Terry Nolan song, resulted in Hugh Barrett's version of the song making the Chicago Top 40. After several years at a station in North Myrtle Beach, South Carolina, Biondi was back in Chicago doing mornings at WBBM-FM in 1983, and then at WJMK-FM in the summer of 1984.

283. "Winkly" was Jim Stagg, who later went to Cleveland, accompanied the Beatles on their first U.S. tour, and then spent years at WCFL-AM in Chicago. "Nutly" was Bobby Mitchell, longtime San Francisco radio personality who was one of the founders of Autumn Records (the label of the Beau Brummels, Sly Stone, Grace Slick, and others). Both Stagg and Mitchell were working at KYA in San Francisco at the time the Winkly–Nutly record (a take-off on NBC-TV's then-popular Chet Huntley-David Brinkley news anchor team) was made.

284. It was the nameplate of a steamroller parked outside the house where the band used to rehearse.

285. Keith Moon. According to Pete Townshend, this recording was a power play on Moon's part. Dissatisfied with the Who's indebtedness and lack of U.S. stature, Moon was considering splitting the band. *Tommy* brought him back.

Smokey Robinson, circa 1961, perfecting his romantic cool. His biggest hit ever, "Tears of a Clown," made number 1 in 1970.

**286.** *Who was the first artist produced by Smokey Robinson for Motown Records?*

---

**287.** *What three major television stars of the sixties also recorded for Motown?*

---

**288.** *Name three artists who performed the theme song of Dick Clark's afternoon TV series "Where the Action Is."*

---

**289.** *What do Levi Stubbs and Diana Ross have in common with Ike and Tina Turner?*

---

**290.** *Which of the Strangeloves, who had a 1965 hit with "I Want Candy," later became a well-known producer?*

286. Mary Wells ("My Guy," "You Beat Me to the Punch"). Robinson went on to work with many more of the label's artists, most successfully with Marvin Gaye, in addition to writing, singing, and producing with his own Miracles.

287. Paul Peterson of "The Donna Reed Show"; Soupy Sales, who first came to prominence in Detroit; and Irene Ryan, the grandmother on TV's "The Beverly Hillbillies."

288. Keith Allison, Paul Revere and the Raiders, and Freddy Cannon.

289. Stubbs, lead singer for the Four Tops, collaborated with Diana Ross and the Supremes on their 1971 rendition of "River Deep—Moutain High." Ike and Tina Turner had a hit with the song five years earlier, in 1966. The song also appeared as a Deep Purple single in 1969.

290. Richard Gottehrer, who produced "My Boyfriend's Back" for the Angels, "Hang on Sloopy" for the McCoys, and Blondie's first album, among many others. The McCoys were actually discovered by the Strangeloves, when Gottehrer and company hit their Ohio hometown on a tour.

**291.** Which of the following was Creedence Clearwater Revival's first number 1 hit?

a. "Proud Mary"
b. "Bad Moon Rising"
c. "Suzi Q"
d. "Fortunate Son"

**292.** The charts are filled with one-hit wonders, artists who have one hit and then are never heard from again. But one duo stands as the ultimate one-hit wonder. Who are they, and why do they deserve that accolade?

**293.** What is the earliest Chuck Berry hit available in true stereo?

**294.** The Peppermint Rainbow had two minor hits in 1969, "Will You Be Staying after Sunday" and "Don't Wake Me Up in the Morning, Michael." The Decca album that included these hits also features a cut called "Green Tambourine," earlier a hit for the Lemon Pipers. What's the most striking thing about the Peppermint Rainbow version of this song?

291. None of these. Although CCR had nine Top 10 hits during 1969–1971, none ever reached the very top. Number 1 records from that period included "In the Year 2525" by Zager and Evans, Ray Stevens's "Everything Is Beautiful," and "Love Theme from Romeo and Juliet" by Henri Mancini.

292. Zager and Evans. A gimmicky pop novelty, "In the Year 2525" was their first record and was, unfathomably, wildly successful, going to number 1 in both the United States and the United Kingdom in 1969. The duo never released another record that even reached the bottom of the Top 100.

293. "Nadine," which was a hit in 1964. Berry's other sixties hits ("No Particular Place to Go," "Little Marie," "You Never Can Tell," "Promised Land," and "Dear Dad") were also available in true stereo, but reissues of all of these songs tend to show up in mono only. Berry reverted back to mono for his 1972 number 1 smash, "My Ding-a-Ling." Berry may be the single fifties artist whose early hits sound worse in stereo, though. Because of reasons described on page 258, the artificial separation of "rechanneled" stereo is especially deadly to Chuck's grooves.

294. The Peppermint Rainbow used the same backing instrumental track as the Lemon Pipers. The connection was producer Paul Leka, who co-wrote "Green Tambourine." The practice of using back tracks for more than one artist is unusual, but it has occurred from time to time. Perhaps the most unusual example is "California Dreamin' ": The Mamas and the Papas backed up Barry McGuire on his second Dunhill album; Dunhill then dumped McGuire's voice and put the song out with a new lead vocal by Papa John Phillips. It was a shrewd move; as good a song as it was, "California Dreamin' " was ill-suited to McGuire's rasp but perfect for the Mamas and the Papas.

**295.** What was Jimi Hendrix's last public performance?

_____

**296.** Who hosted the legendary "T.A.M.I. Show"?

_____

**297.** Originally a blues band, the Architectural Abdabs changed its name in 1966 to one using the last names of two Georgia bluesmen. Who are they now?

_____

**298.** Both Dinah Washington's "What a Diff'rence a Day Makes" (1959) and Friend and Lover's "Reach Out of the Darkness" (1968) are examples of technically mistitled songs, since in neither song does the singer actually sing the printed titles of the songs. What do the singers sing?

_____

**299.** Which artist(s) had Top 40 records on the most labels?

_____

**300.** Which seventies stars emerged from these psychedelic groups?

    a. The Amboy Dukes
    b. The Vagrants
    c. The Nazz
    d. Clear Light
    e. Blues Project

_____

**301.** Name the three stars featured on the original Super Session LP.

**295.** A jam session with Eric Burdon and War at Ronnie Scott's, a London jazz club, in 1970.

**296.** Jan and Dean, on skateboards. They even eked a minor hit out of the title tune, "(Here They Come) From All Over the World." T.A.M.I. stood for Teen-Age Music International.

**297.** Pink Floyd, named for Pink Anderson and Floyd Council.

**298.** Dinah Washington sings "What a difference a day *made*," and Friend and Lover always sing "Reach out *in* the darkness."

**299.** The Beatles had Top 40 hits with seven different labels: Capitol, Apple, Vee-Jay, Tollie, Swan, MGM, and Atco. Four other artists—James Brown, Gladys Knight and the Pips, Neil Diamond, and Cliff Richard—have had Top 40 hits on five different labels.

**300.**  a. Ted Nugent
b. Leslie West (of Mountain; West, Bruce, and Laing)
c. Todd Rungren
d. Danny Kortchmar (of the Section; many sessions as producer and guitarist)
e. Al Kooper

**301.** Al Kooper, Stephen Stills, and Mike Bloomfield. The *Super Session* concept was actually a sort of desperation move on Kooper's part, since at the time he was stuck with a lousy arrangement as a CBS Records A&R man. It paid off with the biggest hit of his performing career.

302. *Only seven songs have reached number 1 while spending as few as ten weeks on the Top 100. Five of these belong to one group. What are the songs?*

303. *During the mid-sixties a well-known radio station featured the following DJs: Bob Lewis, Chuck Leonard, Charlie Greer, and Herb Oscar Anderson. What was this station, where was it, and who were the station's other three air personalities?*

304. *Which members of the Young Rascals were former members of Joey Dee and the Starliters? Name the Rascals' three number 1 hits. What Bob Dylan song did the Rascals ruin on their 1966 album* Collections?

**302.** The Beatles have five: "Can't Buy Me Love," "Eight Days a Week," "Paperback Writer," "Penny Lane," and "The Long and Winding Road." The others are "I Hear a Symphony" by the Supremes and "I'm Henry VIII, I Am" by Herman's Hermits.

---

**303.** The station was, of course, WABC in New York, probably the most listened-to rock & roll station in the world at that particular time, due to New York's huge listening audience and ABC's 50,000-watt clear channel, which blanketed the East Coast at night. The other three jocks were Dan Ingram, Ron Lundy, and "Cousin Brucie" Morrow.

**304.** Eddie Brigati and Gene Cornish were both Starliters, though they weren't on the group's biggest hit, "Peppermint Twist." The Rascals' number 1 hits were "Good Lovin' " (1966), "Groovin' " (1967), and "People Got to Be Free" (1968). "Like a Rolling Stone" appeared on their second LP, where it was eclipsed by more soulful material.

**305.** Who sang the title songs of the following films?

a. Live and Let Die
b. Goodbye Columbus
c. What's New, Pussycat?
d. Don't Make Waves

---

**306.** Who was on drums?

a. The Animals
b. The Association
c. Cream
d. The Band
e. Booker T. and the M.G.s
f. The Byrds
g. The Dave Clark Five
h. Creedence Clearwater Revival
i. Joey Dee and the Starliters
j. The Doors
k. Gerry and the Pacemakers
l. The Hollies
m. The Lovin' Spoonful
n. Manfred Mann
o. Elvis Presley
p. The Jimi Hendrix Experience
q. Mitch Ryder and the Detroit Wheels
r. The Yardbirds
s. The Monkees
t. Herman's Hermits
u. The Rascals
v. Jefferson Airplane
w. The Grateful Dead
x. The Who
y. Led Zeppelin

---

**307.** What was the first Gamble/Huff-produced record to make the Top 10?

---

**308.** One late sixties group started its chart career with four straight RIAA (Recording Institute Association of America)-certified million-selling records. Name the group and its hits.

---

**309.** Eric Clapton is notorious for constantly changing his appearance. In fact, his 1972 album, The History of Eric Clapton, pays homage to his chameleon-like life by displaying at least ten different guises under which he has been photographed. For a while he even had curly hair. Why?

**305.**  a. Paul McCartney
b. The Association
c. Tom Jones
d. The Byrds

---

**306.**  a. John Steel (and later
     Barry Jenkins)
b. Ted Bluechel, Jr.
c. Ginger Baker
d. Levon Helm
e. Al Jackson
f. Mike Clark
g. Dave Clark
h. Doug Clifford
i. Willie Davis
j. John Densmore
k. Freddie Marsden
l. Donald Rathbone
     (and Robert Elliott,
     occasionally)

m. Joe Butler
n. Mike Hugg
o. D. J. Fontana
p. Mitch Mitchell
q. Johnny "Bee" Badanjek
r. Jim McCarty
s. Mickey Dolenz
t. Barry Whitham
u. Dino Danelli
v. Skip Spence
w. Mickey Hartz and
     Bill Kreutzmann
x. Keith Moon (and
     later Kenney Jones)
y. John Bonham

---

**307.**  "Expressway to Your Heart," the Soul Survivors, 1967. The Kenneth Gamble and Leon Huff team went on to create one of the finest seventies pop combines, Philadelphia International Records.

---

**308.**  The Union Gap (later Gary Puckett and the Union Gap) hit with "Woman, Woman," "Young Girl," "Lady Willpower," and "Over You."

---

**309.**  Clapton claims to have gotten a permanent so that he'd look like Bob Dylan.

**310.** *Awards for the quickest exits from the* Billboard *Top 10 (since the Top 100 songs were listed in 1955) go to one song that reached number 7 but was on the Top 100 for just four weeks, and to a song that made number 3 yet stayed around for only six weeks. What are they?*

_____

**311.** *Which of the following double albums holds the distinction of being the first rock double album? The Miracles'* Greatest Hits from the Beginning; Blonde on Blonde, *by Bob Dylan;* Freak Out, *by Frank Zappa and the Mothers of Invention.*

_____

**312.** *In 1969 Jimi Hendrix tried his hand at producing and came up with a single called "Good Old Rock 'n Roll." Name the group that performed it.*

_____

**313.** *Jefferson Starship drummer John Barbata and Monkees producer Chip Douglas both played in one of the few rock bands ever to perform at the White House, in this case at the request of Tricia Nixon. Name the band.*

310. The fastest exit was made by "Nuttin' for Christmas," by Art Mooney with seven-year-old Barry Gordon, in 1955; the song died as soon as Christmas was over. The other quick exit was "They're Coming to Take Me Away, Ha-Haaa!" by Napoleon XIV in 1966. Making number 3 and then disappearing within six weeks was quite an accomplishment (normal chart time for Top 10 records is more than ten weeks), and this one was perhaps a tribute to how obnoxious the record really was and how rapidly radio stations banned it once it became a media controversy. But all good things (in this case, the absence of the record) must end, it seems; the record was re-released in 1973, and it charted again for four weeks.

311. Most record buyers who picked up *Blonde on Blonde* in 1966 would have been shocked to know that the *very* first rock double album had been released the year before by the Miracles. *Freak Out* came later, in 1967.

312. Cat Mother and the All Night News Boys. The group included Bob Smith (vocals, keyboards), Roy Michaels (guitar, bass), Michael Equine (vocals, percussion), Charlie Chin (guitar, banjo), and Larry Packer (guitar, violin, banjo). The group came up with four albums and one other good single, "Can You Dance to It," before folding.

313. The Turtles. Think about this the next time someone tries to defend Flo and Eddie, the current incarnation of Turtles' leaders Howard Kaylan and Marc Volman.

**314.** Name eight rock performers who have posed nude.

_____

**315.** What is unusual about the production of the Smash LP
Double Shot (of My Baby's Love), *by the Swingin'
Medallions?*

_____

**316.** What do the unusual chart histories of the following records
have in common?

    a. "Dedicated to the One I Love" (the Shirelles)
    b. "Sunshine of Your Love" (Cream)
    c. "Get Together" (the Youngbloods)

314. Cass Elliot in the sixties magazine *Cheetah;* Bebe Buell in *Playboy;* Iggy Pop on the *Iggy and Ziggy—Live in Seattle 4/9/77* bootleg; Joni Mitchell on the sleeve of *For the Roses;* John and Yoko on the covers of *Two Virgins* and *Milk and Honey;* David Cassidy in *Rolling Stone;* and Keith Moon in the book *Before I Get Old; The Story of the Who.*

---

315. Two different versions of the 1966 album were pressed. The original version has the original wording of "Double Shot," which includes the lines "worst hangover I ever had," and "She loved me so long and she loved me so hard/I finally passed out in her front yard." (This version of the album, both in mono and stereo, has "She Drives Me Out of My Mind" in large black letters beneath the titles of the album cuts on the front cover.) A later version of the album has some fairly crude overdubs, changing the lyric lines to "the worst morning after I ever had" and "She kissed me so long and she kissed me so hard. . . ."

---

316. They were all unsuccessful on their first chart entries, fell off the Top 100, and then returned to become Top 5 songs. "Dedicated to the One I Love" got no higher than number 83 when it was released in 1959, but it made number 3 two years later. "Sunshine of Your Love" peaked at number 36 and dropped off the charts but roared back a few months later to take number 5. "Get Together," originally the follow-up to the Youngbloods' hit "Grizzly Bear," only reached number 62 on its first try. Almost two years later it was revived and went to number 5.

**317.** When did the composer of "This Diamond Ring" first play organ on a Bob Dylan recording?

**318.** Dino, Desi, and Billy had a number of sixties hits including "I'm a Fool" and "Not the Lovin' Kind." What is Billy's last name and celebrity connection, and what group did he later join?

**319.** Who replaced the following in their respective bands?

    a. Alan Price, the Animals
    b. Jeff Beck, the Yardbirds
    c. Randy Meisner, the Eagles
    d. Martyn Ware, the Human League
    e. Brian Eno, Roxy Music
    f. Eldridge Bryant, the Temptations
    g. David Ruffin, the Temptations
    h. Dick Taylor, the Rolling Stones

**320.** Which artist had Top 40 hits with the largest number of duet partners?

**321.** Bill Drake, a disc jockey on radio stations in San Francisco, Atlanta, and elsewhere, had a big influence on rock & roll radio, but not during his time on the air. What is Drake's major claim to fame?

**317.** In 1965 Al Kooper appeared with Dylan for the first time on "Like a Rolling Stone." Kooper has successfully lived down his composition (sung by Gary Lewis and the Playboys in 1965) and played up his association with Dylan for twenty years. And it's a good thing, since it was Kooper who discovered the late, great Lynyrd Skynyrd in the early seventies.

**318.** Billy's last name is Hinsche. He's Beach Boy guitarist Carl Wilson's brother-in-law. Hinsche joined the Beach Boys in the mid-seventies. Dino's dad is Dean Martin, and Desi is the son of Lucille Ball and Desi Arnaz.

**319.** a. Dave Rowberry
b. Jimmy Page
c. Joe Walsh
d. Ian Burden
e. Eddie Jobson
f. David Ruffin
g. Dennis Edwards
h. Bill Wyman

**320.** Marvin Gaye. In addition to nearly thirty Top 40 hits as a solo act, he had hit duets with Diana Ross, Mary Wells, Tammi Terrell, and Kim Weston.

**321.** Drake is largely responsible for the "less talk, more music" format so popular with Top 40 stations today. In the mid-sixties, as a programming consultant, Drake came up with a formula for minimizing audience tune outs by keeping station jingles short, having the DJs talk only over the beginnings and ends of records, and timing records and commercials with split-second precision to eliminate dead air. Drake's method—known as "Boss Radio," the slogan of flagship station KHJ in Los Angeles—revolutionized rock & roll broadcasting.

322. What's the difference between the version of Simon and Garfunkel's "Sounds of Silence" that appears on the Wednesday Morning 3 AM *LP* and the one that appears on the Sounds of Silence *LP*?

_____

323. Besides their semi-operatic singing voices, what do Bob Dylan and Gary Puckett (of the Union Gap) have in common?

_____

324. What singer/keyboardist produced the Beau Brummels at Autumn Records and later went on to lead a band that had more number 1 singles (three) than any other integrated band?

_____

325. What late sixties group placed its first three chart hits at number 2, spending thirteen weeks each time on the Top 100, yet never reached 1?

_____

326. What English group was successfully sued for libel by British Prime Minister Harold Wilson in 1968?

322. On *Wednesday Morning 3 AM*, "Sounds of Silence" was done as a folk song, with acoustic instruments (guitar and bass), the two voices split onto opposite channels in stereo, and no drums. This was the original version. Producer Tom Wilson, going for a more commercial sound to release as a single, put both voices and the acoustic instruments in the middle of the stereo mix and surrounded them with electric guitar on one side and electric bass and drums on the other. The "electric" version was released as the single that eventually reached number 1. Listening to both versions, it's difficult to believe that they're using the same basic track. (Paul Simon didn't even know what Wilson was up to, incidentally. He was traveling in England at the time.)

323. Hibbing, Minnesota. Puckett was born there and Dylan, although born in Duluth, was raised in Hibbing.

324. Sly Stone, a staff producer at Autumn. Sly quit after recording a psychedelic group over 200 takes before getting anything usable. The band that drove him out of the studio and onto the stage was the Great Society, featuring Grace Slick.

325. Blood, Sweat and Tears placed "You've Made Me So Very Happy," "Spinning Wheel," and "And When I Die" at number 2 in 1969, and never came close to that achievement thereafter. Served David Clayton-Thomas, the world's smarmiest singer, right, too.

326. The Move. It advertised its single "Flowers in the Rain" with postcards of a naked Wilson in the bath. In settlement of the suit, all royalties from the record went to charity.

**327.** The stereo version of "Leader of the Pack" (1964) by the Shangri-Las is the same take as the single, but the stereo version has one line left out of the song. What is it?

**328.** What was Iron Butterfly's 1968 song title "In-A-Gadda-Da-Vida" supposed to mean?

**329.** What was Elvis's final dramatic film? What well-known TV actress co-starred?

**330.** The documentary Elvis on Tour (1972) contains a sequence in which Elvis is seen in scenes from his earlier films kissing a wide assortment of starlets. What well-known director assembled this sequence?

**331.** Name the rock performers who appeared in the following films.

a. Rio Bravo
b. The Fastest Guitar Alive
c. Carnal Knowledge
d. Let's All Make Love in London
e. Catch My Soul
f. Beyond the Valley of the Dolls
g. Polyester
h. Videodrome

**327.** At the beginning of the second verse, the 45 version has the line, "One day my dad said find somebody new." Probably due to the stereo tape being damaged, this line has been edited out of all stereo versions released to date.

**328.** "In the Garden of Eden," if anything.

**329.** *Change of Habit*, with Mary Tyler Moore, 1970. Mary played a nun in mufti who falls in love with Elvis as a noble ghetto doctor, thus inducing a spiritual crisis whose resolution was even more bizarre than the Diet of Worms.

**330.** Martin Scorsese, who was then working as an editor. Scorsese has gone on to make memorable use of rock, not only in his documentary *The Last Waltz*, but in such dramatic features as *Mean Streets*, *Alice Doesn't Live Here Anymore*, and *The King of Comedy*.

**331.** a. Rick Nelson
b. Roy Orbison
c. Art Garfunkel
d. The Rolling Stones
e. Richie Havens
f. Strawberry Alarm Clock
g. Stiv Bators (The Dead Boys)
h. Debbie Harry

**332.** During the Who's May 1969 performance of "Tommy" at New York's Fillmore East, a spectator reaching for the microphone was pummeled by singer Roger Daltrey and guitarist Pete Townshend. What did the hapless victim want to communicate?

**333.** Where did the word discotheque originate?

**334.** Name two ways in which John Wayne altered rock history.

Ringo Starr and Roger Daltrey in *Lisztomania*, 1975.

332. The man, a plainclothes police officer, wanted to inform the group and the audience that the building next door was on fire. Eventually, the concert hall was evacuated. Townshend and Daltrey spent the night in jail and later paid minor fines on charges of assault.

333. It was first heard during World War II in occupied France. Discotheques were secret nightclubs that featured records instead of live bands. This made detection by the Nazis more difficult, since you can take the needle off a record a lot faster than you can dismantle a drum kit.

334. The Searchers took their name from the 1956 John Ford western in which Wayne starred. And Wayne's favorite expression in that film became the title of Buddy Holly and the Crickets' first hit, "That'll Be the Day."

The Chain Reaction, 1968. At left is Steven Tallavico, a.k.a. Steve Tyler, who went on to form one of the most popular bands of the seventies—Aerosmith.

# 6°

# *Blood On The Bluebooks*
## (The Ultimate Bob Dylan Quiz)
## *By Greil Marcus*

This chapter originally appeared in Boston's alternative weekly newspaper, *The Real Paper*, on April 23, 1975 (questions), and June 18, 1975 (answers). It was compiled by Greil Marcus at just about the last moment when anyone could have been obsessed enough to construct such a devious device. (Revisions have been minor, meaning that, for one thing, answers have not been updated.)

The contest was won by Carol Weissbein of Waltham, Massachusetts, who is the "C.W." referred to in the answers.

## QUICKIES

335. *Shortly after its release in June 1966, two pictures were removed from the inside cover art of* Blonde on Blonde *and the title of one of the songs was changed on the label. Describe these changes.*

167

335. Pictures of a dark-haired woman (rumored to be Dylan in drag) and of a girl speaking into Dylan's ear were removed; "Memphis Blues Again" was changed to "Stuck Inside of Mobile with The" (an alteration maintained on Dylan's 1976 live LP *Hard Rain*).

**336.** *Name the drummer who toured the Far East and Europe with Dylan and the Hawks in 1966. Name the singer he left to join Dylan. Name the singer he joined after the tour.*

**337.** *"If You Gotta Go, Go Now" was a minor hit for what band in the United States, and a major hit for Dylan in what country?*

**338.** *Who killed Davey Moore, and when?*

**339.** *In Minnesota, in the early sixties, Dylan often pretended to be Bobby Vee, in whose band he had briefly played piano. What name did Dylan use when playing with Vee? Who did Dylan claim to have played with previously in order to convince Vee to hire him?*

**340.** *Did Dylan write "Puff the Magic Dragon"?*

**341.** *What did Dylan learn in England?*

**342.** *To whom did Dylan say, "I'm not Dylan, you're Dylan"?*

**336.** Mickey Jones; Trini Lopez; Kenny Rogers. (No one got this right.)

**337.** Manfred Mann (uncharted, 1965); France (number 2, 1965).

**338.** Sugar Ramos, in 1962. (No right answers, but we liked J. M. Seiff's: "Nobody killed him. At least nobody would say he did.")

**339.** Elston Gunn; Conway Twitty. (No one got this right.)

**340.** No.

**341.** The guitar riff in "I Shall Be Free Number 10."

**342.** A. J. Weberman.

343. How did Bob Dylan get tuberculosis?

_____

344. What Dylan song has been recorded by both the Beach Boys and the Crystals?

_____

345. What Dylan song has been recorded by the Young Rascals; Sonny and Cher; and Dino, Desi & Billy?

_____

346. What real-life handle was stolen by vandals?

**343.** As Dylan put it in his 1966 *Playboy* interview: "Carelessness. I lost my one true love. I started drinking. The first thing I know, I'm in a card game. Then I'm in a crap game. I wake up in a pool hall. Then this big Mexican lady drags me off the table, takes me to Philadelphia. She leaves me alone in her house, and it burns down. I wind up in Phoenix. I get a job as a Chinaman. I start working in a dime store, and move in with a 13-year-old girl. Then this big Mexican lady from Philadelpia comes in and burns the house down. I go down to Dallas. I get a job as a "before" in a Charles Atlas "before and after" ad. I move in with a delivery boy who can cook fantastic chili and hot dogs. Then this 13-year-old girl from Phoenix comes and burns the house down. The delivery boy—he ain't so mild: he gives her the knife, and the next thing I know I'm in Omaha. It's so cold there, by this time I'm robbing my own bicycles and frying my own fish. I stumble onto some luck and get a job as a carburetor out at the hot-rod races every Thursday night. I move in with a high school teacher who also does a little plumbing on the side, who ain't much to look at, but who's built a special kind of refrigerator that can turn newspaper into lettuce. Everything's going good until the delivery boy shows up and tries to knife me. Needless to say, he burned the house down, and I hit the road. The first guy that picked me up asked me if I wanted to be a star. What could I say?"

**344.** "The Times They Are A-Changin'."

**345.** "Like a Rolling Stone."

**346.** After the release of "Subterranean Homesick Blues," the handle of the water-pump in Woodstock, New York, disappeared.

**347.** What Dylan songs have been recorded by Elvis Presley? What Elvis songs have been recorded by Dylan?

**348.** Who did Dylan once name as his favorite protest singer?

**349.** How many Grammies has Bob won, and for what?

**350.** What is Dylan's younger brother's name? What is the name of the album he produced?

**351.** What is Bob Dylan's mother's present married name?

**352.** What do the covers of Blonde on Blonde and John Wesley Harding have in common?

**353.** In the liner notes to Bob Dylan, "Rabbit Brown" is mentioned as an influence on Dylan. Who is Rabbit Brown?

**354.** Who was the Italian poet from the fifteenth century?

347. Elvis recorded "Tomorrow Is a Long Time" (which Dylan named the cover version he "treasured most") and "Don't Think Twice, It's All Right." Dylan recorded "Can't Help Falling in Love," "A Fool Such As I," "Blue Moon," and "That's All Right," the latter unreleased.

348. Eydie Gorme. (Easy [see *Playboy* interview], but nobody got it.)

349. Two: one for liner notes to Peter, Paul & Mary's 1963 LP *In the Wind;* and one (shared) for the 1972 *Concert for Bangladesh.**

350. David Zimmerman; *Sleep Faster, We Need the Pillow.*

351. Rutman.

352. Dylan is wearing the same jacket on both.

353. Richard "Rabbit" Brown was a New Orleans blues singer who recorded "James Alley Blues," "The Titanic," and "The Legend of the Dunbar Child" for RCA in 1927; Dylan would have heard "James Alley Blues," one of the most unique and affecting blues ever made, on *The Anthology of American Folk Music, Vol. 3, Songs* (Folkways). You should, too.

354. See, this monstrosity can even fool us. The Italian poet referred to in "Tangled Up in Blue" was from the thirteenth century, and contest winner Carol Weissbein, who caught us, concludes it must be Guido Cavalcanti. We conclude Ms. Weissbein is not to be challenged.

*As of April 23, 1975.

# STUMPERS

**355.**  *How many different performances by Dylan of the following songs have been released on official, non-bootleg albums or singles in the United States?*

a. *"Blowin' in the Wind"*
b. *"From a Buick 6"*
c. *"Can You Please Crawl Out Your Window?"*
d. *"Step It Up and Go"*

---

**356.**  *Name at least five people whose faces appear in the tree on the cover of* John Wesley Harding.

---

**357.**  *Name five songs written to or about Dylan. (None by Dylan himself count.)*

---

**358.**  *Name, date, and place three rock bands named for Dylan songs, lyrics, liner note phrases, etc.*

355.  a. Five: on *The Freewheelin' Bob Dylan, Evening Concerts at
Newport, Newport Broadside, The Concert for Bangladesh,* and *Before the Flood.*\*
b. Two: on different versions of *Highway 61 Revisited.*
c. Two: the December 1965 single of the same name, cut
with the Hawks, and the fall 1965 single mistakenly titled
"Positively Fourth Street" (immediately withdrawn and
replaced with the real "Positively Fourth Street"), cut
with the *Highway 61 Revisited* studio band.
d. None.

356.  Carol Weissbein named all four Beatles plus Karl Marx and
Peter Sellers.

357.  C.W. named "To Bobby" (Joan Baez); "A Simple Desultory
Philippic" (Simon & Garfunkel); "American Pie" (Don
McLean); "Dr. Robert" (the Beatles—wrong, but not bad);
and "Positively Wall Street" (National Lampoon). Other
entries included "I Want to Be Bobby's Girl," "Green Tambourine," "Everybody's Somebody's Fool," "Laugh at Me,"
and "Epistle to Dippy." No one mentioned Eric Anderson's
notorious "The Hustler."

358.  Several people listed the Rolling Stones, apparently in all
innocence. J. M. Seiff listed Freddie and the Dreamers
(after "Bob Dylan's Dream") and, brilliantly, the Meters
(after "Don't follow leaders, watch the parking . . ."). C.W.
crapped out. Three proper answers are: Savage Rose, Den-
mark, late sixties to early seventies (from the liner notes to
*Highway 61 Revisited);* Hypnotist Collector, San Jose, 1966
(from "She Belongs to Me"); and Mystery Trend, San Francisco, 1965 (based on a mishearing of the words "mystery
tramp" in "Like a Rolling Stone").

\*Also included on *Bob Dylan at Budokan,* 1979.

**359.** *On what non-Dylan songs were the following Dylan compositions melodically or rhythmically based?*

    a. *"Girl from the North Country"*
    b. *"A Hard Rain's A-Gonna Fall"*
    c. *"Bob Dylan's Dream"*
    d. *"Masters of War"*
    e. *"Don't Think Twice, It's All Right"*
    f. *"Subterranean Homesick Blues"*
    g. *"Desolation Row"*
    h. *"Like a Rolling Stone"*

**360.** *Describe the actions of the following in various Dylan songs.*

    a. *Beethoven*
    b. *Shakespeare*
    c. *Einstein*
    d. *John F. Kennedy*
    e. *Richard Burton*
    f. *Olatunji*
    g. *Rock-a-day Johnny*
    h. *Barry Goldwater*
    i. *Moby Dick*
    j. *Tom Paine*

# ESSAY QUESTIONS (50 WORDS OR LESS)

**361.** *What is the worst thing Bob Dylan has ever done?*

**362.** *What is the best thing Bob Dylan has ever done?*

**359.**   a. "Scarborough Fair" (the Child ballad, not the Simon and
           Garfunkel version)
   b. "Lord Randall"
   c. "Lord Franklin's Dream"
   d. "Notamun Town"
   e. "Understand Your Man"
   f. "Too Much Monkey Business"
   g. "El Paso"
   h. "La Bamba"

(The last two were hard, but no one even tried.)

**360.**   a. Unwraps a bedroll with Ma Rainey.
   b. Speaks to a French girl in an alley.
   c. Disguises himself as Robin Hood, bums a cigarette, sniffs
      drainpipes, recites the alphabet, and once played electric
      violin.
   d. Telephones Dylan for advice on how to make the country
      grow.
   e. Reprimands Dylan for making love to Elizabeth Taylor.
   f. Is barred from making shaving cream commercials be-
      cause he is non-white.
   g. Sings "Tell your ma, tell your pa, our love is gonna grow,
      oo-wah, oo-wah."
   h. Is refused permission to move in next door to Dylan or
      marry his daughter.
   i. Marries the deputy sheriff.
   j. Rescues the singer from a fair young maiden.

**361.**   C.W.: "His recording of 'Spanish Is the Loving Tongue' on
       *Dylan*."

**362.**   C.W.: "Visions of Johanna"

**363.**   What is the most mediocre thing Bob Dylan has ever done?

_____

**364.**   What is the most outrageous thing Bob Dylan has ever done?

_____

**365.**   What is the least outrageous thing Bob Dylan has ever done?

_____

**366.**   What is the dumbest and/or most pretentious piece of writing ever produced about Bob Dylan?

_____

**367.**   What is the dumbest and/or most pretentious piece of writing ever produced by Bob Dylan?

**363.** C.W.: *"Self Portrait.* The album is not absolutely terrible, as some people think, and the idea behind it is pretty good. It is mediocre because it has some good songs, some awful ones, and consists mostly of un-outstanding renditions of un-outstanding songs."

**364.** C.W. says it was Dylan's posing in drag on the cover of *Bringing It All Back Home.* He didn't, though; the woman was Sally Grossman, the then-wife of Dylan's then-manager Albert Grossman.

Beiber Archives: "He tied Levon Helm's shoelaces together, then asked the boys in the Band to come forward and take a bow."

Our answer: Telling Mick Jagger that he, Dylan, could have written "Satisfaction" but that Jagger could never have written "Like a Rolling Stone" (or was it "Mr. Tambourine Man"?).

**365.** C.W.: " 'One Too Many Mornings.' It has no 'bad rhymes,' which embarrass novitiate Dylan fans, is 'folkie' enough for his folk fans, makes no political or social comments to anger anyone, and does not even contain the usual antagonism toward the lover but is rather conciliatory."

**366.** By consensus, Toby Tyler's *Positively Main Street.* (This contest got a couple of votes, too.)

**367.** C.W.: " 'The Ballad of Donald White' (unreleased). It has more stilted sentences and bad rhymes than most of Dylan's early songs and is only a bare restatement of the criminals-are-society's-victims cliché without the insight Dylan usually provides."

**368.** What is the best drug reference in a Dylan song?

_____

**369.** What is the best reference to perversion in a Dylan song?

_____

**370.** What is the best political reference in a Dylan song?

_____

**371.** Who is greater, Bob Dylan or Elvis Presley? Why?

**368.** C.W.: " 'Six white horses' in 'Absolutely Sweet Marie,' partially for its relative obscurity, but mostly because as part of the song it creates a good paradox—drugs delivered to a man already in prison—which parallels the following paradox of the outlaw's necessary honesty."

---

**369.** C.W.: "The fourth verse of 'Highway 61 Revisited,' because it is elegant and compact. Along with its implications of incest, it employs an allusion to *Twelfth Night*, in which a woman falls in love with a girl disguised as a boy and tries to seduce 'him'."

---

**370.** C.W.: "The verse referring to 'The vice president's gone mad' in 'Talking Clothesline Blues.' Written in 1967, before Nixon and Agnew were elected, it was uncannily prophetic of events to come and very perceptive about what the average person's attitude toward the political scandal would be." Very nice—but in 1967 *Hubert Humphrey* was crazy as a loon.

---

**371.** C.W.: "Although 'Zimmerman' could not have become 'Dylan' had not Presley preceded him, Dylan is greater. His talents cover a wider scope, and his influence has been broader. Presley was an unbelievable singer, but Dylan is also a poet and a prophet in the true biblical tradition of social criticism."

Beiber Archives argues: "Elvis is greater, because he married his childhood sweetheart, calls total strangers 'Sir' (or 'Suh'), knows karate, can eat ten ice cream bars at one sitting, and does not know Bill Graham from Tommy Sands."

From an unsigned entry: "Elvis. He has a bigger gun collection."

**372.** *What do Dylan and Benny Goodman have in common?*

_____

**373.** *When did Dylan sell out? (Strict accuracy required.)*

# MIND BOGGLERS

**374.** *Name all officially released Dylan performances that have never appeared on official albums.**

_____

**375.** *Name all songs from* The Basement Tapes *on which Dylan sings lead.*

_____

**376.** *For each song on* The Basement Tapes *sung by Dylan, name another performer who has recorded it. (Obscurities will be favored.)*

_____

*As of April 23, 1975

372. Both came from middle-class Jewish families. Both have first names beginning with "B" and (originally) last names ending with "man." And, adds Henry Armetta, "neither of them swings."

373. C.W.: "Dylan never sold out, though his New York concerts of last year did."

    Actually, he sold out for the first time in 1982, when he allowed Bill Graham to convince him to drop his all-Christian concert repertoire for a mix of religious songs and greatest hits.

374. "Mixed-Up Confusion"; "Can You Please Crawl Out Your Window" (two versions); "If You Gotta Go, Go Now"; "Spanish Is the Loving Tongue" (version from the flipside of "Watching the River Flow"); "George Jackson" (two versions); "Just Like Tom Thumb's Blues" (live version).

375. "Million Dollar Bash"; "Yea! Heavy and a Bottle of Bread"; "Please, Mrs. Henry"; "Down in the Flood (Crash on the Levee)"; "Lo and Behold!"; "Tiny Montgomery"; "Too Much of Nothing"; "Tears of Rage"; "This Wheel's on Fire"; "The Mighty Quinn (Quinn the Eskimo)"; "Nothing Was Delivered"; "Open the Door, Richard (Homer)"; "Apple Suckling Tree"; "Talking Clothesline Blues"; "I'm Not There (I'm Gone)"; "Odds and Ends"; "Get Your Rocks Off"; "I Shall Be Released"; "You Ain't Goin' Nowhere"; "Sign on the Cross"; "Goin' to Acapulco."

376. No complete list of answers; something must be left to the imagination, or the next contest. C.W. scored heavily with her discovery of a version of "I'm Not There (I'm Gone)" by Shirley Bassey, of all people.

**377.** Name all Rolling Stones songs clearly influenced by Bob Dylan.

_____

**378.** Name all Monkees songs clearly influenced by Dylan.

_____

**379.** List 100 Dylan recordings that remain unreleased.*

_____

**380.** List all references to rain in Dylan's compositions.

_____

**381.** List all references to Italy and Italians in Dylan compositions.

_____

**382.** List all American place names in Dylan compositions.

_____

*As of April 23, 1975

377. No one did well on this one. Obvious entries would include "Who's Been Sleeping Here," "Something Happened to Me Yesterday," "Get Off of My Cloud," "19th Nervous Breakdown," "Sitting on a Fence," and "Where the Boys Are."

378. Everyone chose "Last Train to Clarksville." What about "Pleasant Valley Sunday"?

379. There are far more than 100, so we will merely reprint C.W.'s list: 1. "The Death of Emmett Till"; 2. "The Ballad of Donald White"; 3. "Candy Man"; 4. "Baby Please Don't Go"; 5. "Hard Times in New York Town"; 6. "Poor Lazarus"; 7. "It's Hard to Be Blind"; 8. "Dink's Song"; 9. "Omie Wise"; 10. "Wade in the Water"; 11. "I Was Young When I Left Home"; 12. "Sally Gal"; 13. "Long John"; 14. "Cocaine"; 15. "VD Blues"; 16. "VD Waltz"; 17. "VD City"; 18. "VD Gunner's Blues"; 19. "Black Cross"; 20. "Stealin' "; 21. "Jesus Met the Woman at the Well"; 22. "Gypsy Davy"; 23. "Pastures of Plenty"; 24. "Jesse James"; 25. "Remember Me"; 26. "San Francisco Bay Blues"; 27. "I'd Hate to Be You on That Dreadful Day"; 28. "Walking Down the Line"; 29. "Train A-Travelin' "; 30. "Cuban Blockade"; 31. "All Over You"; 32. "Fare Thee Well (The Leaving of Liverpool)"; 33. "Man on the Street"; 34. "He Was a Friend of Mine"; 35. "Talking Bear Mountain Picnic Massacre Blues"; 36. "Car Car"; 37. "Pretty Polly"; 38. "Only a Hobo"; 39. "Babe I'm in the Mood for You"; 40. "Quit Your Lowdown Ways"; 41. "John Brown"; 42. "Paths of Victory"; 43. "Seven Curses"; 44. "Mama, You Been on My Mind"; 45. "I'll Keep It with Mine"; 46. "Denise, Denise"; 47. "New Orleans Rag (103)"; 48. "East Laredo"; 49. "I've Been a Moonshiner (The Bottle Song)"; 50. "The Eternal Circle"; 53. "Lay Down Your Weary Tune"; 54. "Who Killed Davey Moore?"; 55. "Tell Me Mama (What's Wrong with You)"; 56–77. The Basement Tapes, as in Answer 375;

78. "Medicine Society"; 79. "Hero Blues"; 80. "Worried Blues"; 81. "Lonesome Whistle Blues"; 82. "Fill-in-the-Blank Blues"; 83. "Wichita Blues"; 84. "Milkcow Calf's Blues"; 85. "I Wanna Be Your Lover"; 86. "She's Your Lover Now"; 87. "Folsom Prison Blues"; 88. "East Virginia"; 89. "Ring of Fire"; 90. "Wild Mountain Thyme"; 91. "Talking Devil"; 92. "Acne"; 93. "Barbed Wire Fence"; 94. "On the Trail of the Buffalo"; 95. "Seventy Dollar Robbery"; 96. "Ain't Gonna Grieve"; 97. "Barbara Allen"; 98. "Gypsy Lou"; 99. "Trail of the Buffalo"; 100. "East Orange N.J."

Just for fun, we'll add these numbers cut with Johnny Cash in 1969: "Mountain Dew"; "I Still Miss Someone"; "Careless Love"; "Matchbox"; "That's All Right Mama"; "Big River"; "I Walk the Line"; "You Are My Sunshine"; "I Guess Things Happen That Way"; "Just a Closer Walk with Thee"; "T for Texas." The most closely guarded of all unreleased Dylan numbers are the tracks cut with the Rolling Stones; we have not even heard tell of what songs were put down, let alone what they sound like. And this is not even to mention the legendary "Million Dollar Quartet" session, cut in 1957 with Elvis Presley, Carl Perkins, and Jerry Lee Lewis.

---

380. C.W.:

1. "Amidst a bloody red rain"—"Emmett Till"
2. "A Hard Rain's A-Gonna Fall"
3. "Like a dirty, drivin' rain"—"Hollis Brown"
4. "Turn, turn to the rain and the wind"—"Percy's Song"
5. "Oh, the cruel rain and the wind"—"Percy's Song"
6. "As the echo of the wedding bells before the blowin' rain"—"Chimes of Freedom"
7. "The rain-unraveled tales"—"Chimes of Freedom"
8. "Fold my hands and pray for rain"—"Maggie's Farm"
9. "Everybody's makin' love or else expecting rain"—"Desolation Row"

10. "Noah's great rainbow"—"Desolation Row"
11. "The night blows cold and rainy"—"Love Minus Zero/ No Limit"
12. "When you're lost in the rain in Juarez"—"Just Like Tom Thumb's Blues"
13. "Rainy Day Women #12 & 35"
14. "Louise holds a handful of rain"—"Visions of Johanna"
15. "The harmonicas play/The skeleton keys and the rain"— "Visions of Johanna"
16. "Now, the rainman gave me two cures"—"Memphis Blues Again"
17. "Tonight as I stand inside the rain"—"Just Like a Woman"
18. "It was raining from the first"—"Just Like a Woman"
19. "Well, the rainman comes in with his magic wand"—"I Wanna Be Your Lover"
20. "And the rainman leaves in the wolfman's disguise"—"I Wanna Be Your Lover"
21. "Rain won't lift"—"You Ain't Goin' Nowhere," *The Basement Tapes*
22. "Clouds so swift and rain fallin' in"—"You Ain't Goin' Nowhere," *Bob Dylan's Greatest Hits, Vol. 2*
23. "Whose tears are like rain"—"I Pity the Poor Immigrant"
24. "Rain would gather too"—"If Not For You"
25. "Two mules, trains, and rain"—"If Dogs Run Free"
26. "Looks like nothin' but rain"—"Sign on the Window"
27. "Father of Love and Father of Rain"—"Father of Night"
28. "Rainy days on the Great Lakes"—"Something There Is about You"
29. "Rain fallin' on my shoes"—"Tangled Up in Blue"
30. "I'm back in the rain"—"You're a Big Girl Now"
31. "Buckets of Rain"

There must be more, but this is a heroic answer. (You didn't think *we* knew, did you?)

**381.** C.W.:

1. "Lord, she took it away to Italy—Italy"—"Down the Highway"
2. Sophia Loren in "I Shall Be Free"
3. Galileo in "Tombstone Blues"
4. Romeo in "Desolation Row"
5. Nero in "Desolation Row"
6. The Mona Lisa in "Visions of Johanna"
7. "Oh, the streets of Rome/Are filled with rubble"— "When I Paint My Masterpiece"
8. Botticelli—"When I Paint My Masterpiece"
9. "An Eye-talian poet from the 13th century!"—"Tangled Up in Blue"
10. "They say I shot a man named Gray/And took his wife to Italy"—"Idiot Wind"

Again, there must be more, but who knows where?

---

**382.** Both C.W. and Fred Shapiro turned in superb answers, C.W. by song, Shapiro by place. We follow Shapiro's answer, which omits duplications of places mentioned in more than one song.

Alabama: Mobile
Arizona: Grand Canyon
Arkansas
California: San Francisco, Cannery Row
Colorado: Denver, Cripple Creek
Florida: Tallahassee
Georgia
Hawaii: Honolulu
Idaho
Illinois: Chicago, Joliet Prison
Kansas: Wichita
Louisiana: Shreveport, Baton Rouge, New Orleans

Maryland: Baltimore
Minnesota: Duluth, North Country
Mississippi: Oxford, Jackson
Missouri: Kansas City
Montana
Nebraska: Omaha
Nevada: Las Vegas
New Jersey: East Orange
New Mexico: Albuquerque, Santa Fe, Taos
New York State: Washington Heights, Greenwich Village, Statue of Liberty, Bowery, Staten Island, 42nd Street, Spanish Harlem, Tenth Avenue, Fourth Street, Broadway, Harlem, Brooklyn, New York City, Syracuse, Buffalo
North Carolina: Thomasville
Ohio: Ashtabula
Oklahoma
Oregon
Pennsylvania: Pittsburgh
South Dakota
Texas: Chaney County, Abilene, San Antonio, El Paso
Utah
Virginia: Gallus Road, Arlington
Washington: Seattle
Wyoming: Cheyenne
Others: Brighton, Mississippi River, Williamspoint, Delacroix, Blueberry Hill, Mink Muscle Creek, Rocky Mountains, Highway 61

# BONUS QUESTIONS

*383.* What was Bob Dylan's oddest habit as a teenager?

_____

*384.* In the unreleased Dylan composition "Percy's Song" (recorded by Fairport Convention), the singer's friend receives a sentence of ninety-nine years in Joliet Prison for "highest degree" manslaughter. What is the maximum penalty for voluntary or first-degree manslaughter in the relevant state?

383.  He took up to a dozen showers a day.

---

384.  The state is Illinois; C.W. cites a penalty of fifteen years. When we called the Illinois Department of Corrections to check, they said it depended. Depended on what, we asked. On what the judge had for breakfast, they said.

# 7

# *Days Of Future Passed—Out From Boredom*
## (The Seventies)

385. *Original bassist (and chief songwriter) Glen Matlock was acknowledged to be the best musician in the Sex Pistols. Under what circumstances did he leave the band?*

386. *What is the connection between the Beach Boys and Barry Manilow?*

387. *Briefly describe the Beach Boys' relationship to the Republican Party.*

193

**385.** He was fired for "liking the Beatles." His place was taken by Sid Vicious, who wasn't such a sissy and who also couldn't play the bass.

---

**386.** Beach Boy Bruce Johnston wrote Barry's 1976 hit "I Write the Songs."

---

**387.** In 1980 the band aided ex-CIA chief George Bush's presidential campaign. Meanwhile, Beach Boy Mike "Baldie" Love has become an occasional dinner companion of Watergate strongman G. Gordon Liddy, and various members of the once-great group have posed with the Mad Bomber of Grenada and Nancy at the White House.

**388.** Elton John's period of greatest popularity was the mid-seventies. What unprecedented feat did the two albums he issued in 1975 achieve on the record charts?

**389.** Who played keyboards on "You Can't Always Get What You Want"?

**390.** What was the first group to receive royalties from records sold in the U.S.S.R.?

**391.** Name the first American band to play the Soviet Union. For extra credit, what popular singer/songwriter was briefly a member of that band in the sixties? Which of his hits featured Russians?

**392.** Which rock festival had the largest attendance ever?

**393.** In which films were the following songs featured?

   a. "The First Time Ever I Saw Your Face," Roberta Flack
   b. "Mrs. Robinson," Simon and Garfunkel
   c. "Darling Be Home Soon," the Lovin' Spoonful
   d. "Sisters of Mercy," Leonard Cohen
   e. "Call Me," Blondie
   f. "Ballad of Lucy Jordan," Marianne Faithful
   g. "Jesus Is Just Alright," the Byrds
   h. "Tender Years," Beaver Brown
   i. "All the Way to Memphis," Mott the Hoople
   j. "Tell Me," the Rolling Stones
   k. "Who Are You," the Who

**388.** Both *Captain Fantastic & the Brown Dirt Cowboy* and *Rock of the Westies* entered the LP charts at number 1. His popularity in 1974 must have been somewhat less, since his two LPs released that year each took one week to make number 1.

**389.** No, not Nicky Hopkins. It was Al Kooper.

**390.** The Rolling Stones were the first to benefit from the change in Soviet copyright laws in 1975.

**391.** The Nitty Gritty Dirt Band, which featured Jackson Browne as a member on one early single. Browne's 1983 hit, "Lawyers in Love," attacks the 1980s Cold War by making all the Russians on earth disappear.

**392.** Watkins Glen Summer Jam, New York City, July 28, 1973. Six hundred thousand people showed up. Woodstock attendance was officially recorded at a mere 400,000, throwing into question Joni Mitchell's estimation, "We were half a million strong."* Watkins Glen, a one-day affair, featured the Grateful Dead, the Band, and the Allman Brothers Band.

*Not surprisingly, Mitchell never appeared at Woodstock.

**394.** Which famous recording acts recorded under the following aliases?

    a. Suzy and the Red Stripes
    b. Dib Cochran and the Earwigs
    c. The Dumbbells
    d. Klark Kent
    e. The Imposter

_____

**395.** What song on the Band's *Cahoots* album contains a guest vocal by Van Morrison?

_____

**396.** *Cahoots* also featured the Band's last studio recording of a Dylan song. What was it?

_____

**397.** What do the following have in common:

    a. Chuck Berry
    b. Arlo Guthrie
    c. Paul McCartney
    d. Chrissie Hynde

**393.** a. *Play Misty for Me* (1971)
b. *The Graduate* (1967)
c. *You're a Big Boy Now* (1966)
d. *McCabe and Mrs. Miller* (1971)
e. *American Gigolo* (1980)
f. *Montenegro* (1981)
g. *Easy Rider* (1969)
h. *Eddie and the Cruisers* (1983)
i. *Alice Doesn't Live Here Anymore* (1975)
j. *Mean Streets* (1973)
k. *Bad Timing: A Sensual Obsession* (1980)

**394.** a. Wings
b. Marc Bolan and David Bowie
c. Roxy Music
d. Stewart Copeland (of the Police)
e. Elvis Costello

**395.** "Four Percent Pantomime." The title is a reference to the difference in alcoholic content between Johnny Walker Red and Black. Van was briefly the Band's neighbor in Woodstock, where they presumably studied the difference.

**396.** "When I Paint My Masterpiece," which also appeared on Dylan's *Greatest Hits, Vol. 2.*

**397.** They have all spent time in prison.

**398.** *What distinction do these performers share?*

a. Bob Dylan
b. Ian Hunter
c. Patti Smith
d. Jim Carroll
e. Jim Morrison
f. Charlie Watts
g. John Lennon
h. Bette Midler
i. George Harrison

**399.** *What do these bands have in common?*

a. The Atlanta Rhythm Section
b. Delaney and Bonnie and Friends
c. Mad Dogs and Englishman
d. MFSB
e. The Muscle Shoals Horns

**400.** *What does this motley crew share?*

a. Benny Goodman
b. Bruce Springsteen
c. Count Basie
d. Charlie Christian
e. Aretha Franklin
f. Bob Dylan

**401.** *What platinum-selling R&B band began its professional career as Leon Russell's backup band?*

**402.** *What was Chicago's twelfth album called?*

**403.** *Name Paul Simon's first solo hit and the inspiration for its title.*

199

**398.** They have all written books:

    a. *Tarantula*
    b. *Diary of a Rock and Roll Star* (or *Reflections of a Rock and Roll Star*, as it was titled in the United States)
    c. *Seventh Heaven* and *Babel*
    d. *The Basketball Diaries* and *Living at the Movies*
    e. *The Lords and the New Creatures*
    f. *Ode to a High-Flying Bird*
    g. *In His Own Write*
    h. *A View From a Broad* and *The Saga of Baby Divine*
    i. *I Me Mine*

**399.** All emerged from session work.

**400.** They were all discovered by talent scout John Hammond, Jr.

**401.** The Gap Band, in their (and Leon's) hometown, Tulsa, Oklahoma.

**402.** *Hot Streets.* Maybe they weren't sure if twelve was "XII" or "XIIX."

**403.** "Mother and Child Reunion." The title is derived from an item on a menu in a Chinese restaurant, an egg and chicken dish.

The Monkees, 1966.

---

**404.** *What is the connection between the Monkees and Kansas?*

---

**405.** *What is the only cover song recorded by Steely Dan?*

---

**406.** *In 1974, B. B. King had a Top 30 hit with a song written by one of Motown's greatest superstars. What was the song and who was its composer?*

---

**407.** *Under what name did Robbie Krieger and John Densmore record during the early seventies, after the dissolution of the Doors?*

---

**408.** *The Country Hams never even made the charts with their 1974 single "Walking in the Park with Eloise," but they did enjoy great success under another name. Who were the Country Hams?*

**404.** Don Kirshner, who assembled the Monkees, also signed Kansas to his Kirshner label. We leave it to you to infer the musical connection.

**405.** Duke Ellington's "East St. Louis Toodle-oo" on *Pretzel Logic*. However, there are also those who'd argue for the strong resemblance between their final LP, *Gaucho*, and the wallpaper jazz of Keith Jarrett.

**406.** "I Like to Live the Love," by Stevie Wonder. Although King has released dozens of singles, many of which made the Top 10 on the soul charts, the classic guitarist's only other Top 30 pop hit was 1969's "The Thrill Is Gone."

**407.** The Butts Band, which also featured some of the players in Rod Stewart's post-Faces group.

**408.** Wings. The record didn't get any air play, either, but it hardly mattered to Paul. He recorded the song as a lark; his father had written it many years before.

**409.** *Aside from throwing up at airports, trashing their record companies' offices, saying "fuck" on TV, and singing songs about anarchy and the worthlessness of the Queen, the Sex Pistols were well-known and vilified for their appearance, which launched a million Mohawks and ripped T-shirts. Malcolm McLaren, the entrepreneur who carefully orchestrated most aspects of the Pistols' career, was responsible for their fashion trend setting as well. Where did he get the idea for spiky hair and ripped T-shirts?*

---

**410.** *The following ad appeared in* Melody Maker *in August 1975: "Wanted: whiz kid guitarist. Not older than 20, not worse looking than Johnny Thunder. . . ." What was it for, and what were the results?*

Meisterhyper
Malcolm
McLaren,
whose
talent for
exploitation
knows no
bounds.

**409.** Although McLaren and his wife, Vivienne Westwood, ran a fashionable boutique, their fashion sense wasn't that perceptive. While Malcolm was managing the New York Dolls, he saw Richard Hell play with Television in New York in 1975. He was struck by Hell's short hair and ripped T-shirts, a style no one else at the time was affecting, and asked Hell if he could manage him. Hell refused, McLaren and the Dolls soon parted company, and McLaren formed the Pistols soon afterward. Pistols Johnny Rotten and Glen Matlock once personally apologized to Hell for stealing his looks and his riffs. Not that they didn't improve upon them. . . .

---

**410.** It was placed by Malcolm McLaren for his new group, you-know-who. The response was overwhelming, but McLaren eventually chose a young man named John Lydon, who worked in his shop. He didn't play guitar but he surely did sing, in his way. The rest is well-known.

**411.** *Why doesn't Earth, Wind and Fire include Water?*

_____

**412.** *What British artist, by mid-1976, had placed no fewer than seventy-one songs in the British Top 40 yet could do no better than one Top 10 hit in the States?*

_____

**413.** *When Pete Townshend performed at a benefit concert for the Rock Against Racism organization in London in July 1979, he was backed by a band that featured harp player Peter Hope-Evans, bassist Tony Butler, and two new Who members, drummer Kenney Jones and keyboardist John "Rabbit" Bundrick. How was the Who's main man accompanied at his only previous solo show, five years earlier?*

_____

**414.** *There is no group name indicated on the cover of the first Genesis album. Why?*

_____

**415.** *Match the lead singer with his group:*

a. The Four Tops         1. Ron Banks
b. The Dramatics         2. Philip Bailey
c. The Dells             3. Errol Brown
d. The Stylistics          4. Tony Williams
e. Hot Chocolate         5. Marvin Junior
f. Shalamar              6. Russell Thompkins
g. The Platters           7. Charles Wilson
h. The Gap Band         8. James "J.T." Taylor
i. Earth, Wind and Fire    9. Levi Stubbs
j. Kool and the Gang      10. Howard Hewett

411. Maurice White named the band for the predominant elements in his astrological chart, which is dry.

412. Cliff Richard, for some reason, did not sell well in the United States until late 1976, when "Devil Woman" went to number 6. Since then he's had a number of Top 40 hits, including "We Don't Talk Anymore" and "Dreaming," which both made the Top 10. After more than seventy Top 40 hits in England, his 1976 album was titled *I'm Nearly Famous*.

413. Musical backing for the benefit show at London's Roundhouse in 1974 was supplied by an assortment of tapes made at Townshend's home studio. The versatile musician handled piano and acoustic and electric guitars live. Prior to playing a one-man band version of "My Generation," Townshend played a series of self-made demo tapes of the 1965 hit for the appreciative audience. (One take of the home-grown rendition can be heard on the flexi-disc included with

413. Richard Barnes's book *The Who: Maximum R&B*.)

414. Decca, which signed the group, wanted it to change its name because an American group called Genesis already existed. The group and its then-manager, Jonathan King (the Howard Cosell of British music), refused, but King eventually worked out a compromise. The LP was titled *From Genesis to Revelation*, and no group name was given. The 1969 album was a concept LP that Peter Gabriel described as "Terribly pretentious . . . the history of man's evolution in ten simple pop songs."

415. a—9; b—1;c—5;d—6;e—3; f—10; g—4; h—7; i—2; j—8.

**416.** Tuning in the radio in 1970, one was likely to hear any of three different versions of the Free hit "All Right Now." Explain.

_____

**417.** Director Nicholas Roeg often uses rock stars as actors in his films. Name three that he's featured and the Roeg films in which they star.

_____

**418.** Almost every contemporary R&B singer can claim roots in gospel music. Match each of the following artists with the gospel group in which he or she sang.

a. Lou Rawls                1. The Violinaires
b. Sam Cooke                2. The Meditation Singers
c. Wilson Pickett           3. The Pilgrim Travelers
d. Cissy Houston            4. The New Bethel Baptist
e. Aretha Franklin             Church Choir
f. Laura Lee                5. The Soul Stirrers
                            6. The Drinkard Singers

**416.** The single, LP, and DJ versions of "All Right Now" all had different lengths. The album version ran 5:32, and an edited DJ version ran about 3:29. The commercial single, on the other hand, was a completely different mix of the song, with still a different edit, running about 4:20. All three versions received air play.

---

**417.** Mick Jagger, *Performance;* David Bowie, *The Man Who Fell to Earth;* and Art Garfunkel, *Bad Timing: A Sensual Obsession.*

---

**418.** a—3; b—5; c—1; d—6; e—4; f—2.

Sam Cooke, one of rock's greatest singers and among the first to own a record label, Sar.

**419.** Name the only member of the Who who toured as a solo act.

_____

**420.** What American musician who later graced several Who albums played most of the keyboards on Catch a Fire, the 1972 breakthrough reggae album by Bob Marley and the Wailers?

_____

**421.** Name the products for which the following hits became commercials.

   a. "Good Vibrations," by the Beach Boys
   b. "Just One Look," by Doris Troy
   c. "Hold on Tight," by Electric Light Orchestra
   d. "Breaking Up Is Hard to Do," by Neil Sedaka
   e. "Leader of the Pack," by the Shangri-Las
   f. "Woman," by Peter and Gordon
   g. "Splish Splash," by Bobby Darin
   h. "Oh, Pretty Woman," by Roy Orbison
   i. "We Are Family," by Sister Sledge

_____

**422.** Which of the following groups did David Bowie not belong to?

   a. The Conrads
   b. The King Bees
   c. The Lower Third
   d. The Outcasts
   e. The Buzz

_____

**423.** Who billed themselves in 1975 as "The Guys That Wrote 'Em and the Guys Who Sung 'Em" for a short-lived tour?

**419.** Bassist John Entwistle took a five-piece band, Ox (after his own nickname), on a three-month tour of England and America in early 1975 after the release of his fourth record, *Mad Dog*. The reviews of the album and the shows, and especially the losses incurred presenting the concerts, put a halt to Entwistle's solo career for six years.

**420.** John "Rabbit" Bundrick, a Texas native who lived in London and recorded a couple of solo LPs for Marley's label, Island Records.

**421.** a. Sunkist orange soda
b. Mazda
c. National Coffee Association
d. Burger King
e. McDonald's Big Mac
f. Enjoli Cologne
g. GTE Flip Phone
h. Sasson jeans
i. Pepsi Free

**422.** The Outcasts, which was a precursor of the Small Faces, containing Ronnie Lane and Kenney Jones.

**423.** Tommy Boyce, Bobby Hart, Mickey Dolenz, and Davy Jones. Hart and Boyce wrote several of the Monkees' hits, including "Last Train to Clarksville." Dolenz and Jones were the Monkees who sang 'em.

? and the Mysterians with Bob Gallo of Talentmasters Recording Studios. The band had a hit with "96 Tears" in 1966.

424. *What are the real names of the following?*

  *a. Lobo*
  *b. M*
  *c. ? of the Mysterians*

  _____

425. *What platinum single did Rod Temperton write for his own group before moving on to write hits for Michael Jackson?*

  _____

426. *Which songs did Rod Temperton write for Jackson?*

  _____

427. *In 1975 Pete Wingfield released a song called "Eighteen with a Bullet." How well did it do?*

  _____

428. *The lead singer of the Rotary Connection, a group famous for its sixties psychedelic ballads, had a number 1 hit of her own in 1975 with "Lovin' You." Who was she?*

1983's phenomenon before puberty and nose job.

**424.** a. Kent Lavoie
b. Robin Scott
c. Rudy Martinez

**425.** Heatwave's "Boogie Nights" (1977).

**426.** Temperton's *Off the Wall* credits include "Off the Wall," "Rock with You," and "Burn This Disco Out." He wrote "Baby Be Mine," "The Lady in My Life," and "Thriller" for *Thriller*.

**427.** It made number 15. Along the way it spent a week at eighteen with a bullet, though some suspected the trade-paper chart of making allowances for the history books.

**428.** Minnie Riperton. She died on July 12, 1979.

**429.** *What was the first black group to win a Grammy for a country record?*

_____

**430.** *Apart from the* Layla *sessions, Derek and the Dominoes cut one studio single. Who was its producer?*

_____

**431.** *A live rendition of "Won't Get Fooled Again" is used as the finale to the 1979 Who rockumentary* The Kids Are Alright. *What is unique about this segment?*

_____

**432.** *Name the American composers who wrote the following hits for Deep Purple:*

a. *"Hush"*
b. *"Kentucky Woman"*
c. *"River Deep—Mountain High"*

The Nazz's only smash, "Hello It's Me," became a hit three years later in 1973 for its skinny front man, Todd Rundgren (at left).

Shepherd's Bush favorites, the Who, in 1963.

**429.** The Pointer Sisters, for "Fairytale" in 1975.

---

**430.** Phil Spector. The song was "Tell the Truth." It's included in the Atco album *The History of Eric Clapton*.

---

**431.** The version of the song that ends the picture was filmed during the Who's second performance of it at a special May 1978 show held in the band's own Shepperton Studios. *Kids* compiler/director Jeff Stein requested the extra take at the end of the concert, held for the purposes of capturing some "definitive" live performances. Pete Townshend, enraged at the idea of hitting the boards again (at a time when he otherwise eschewed all live performances), went out and delivered a bravura performance that simultaneously recalled and parodied his finest stage moments. After smashing his guitar to the floor one last time, Townshend helped Keith Moon over his drum kit and hugged the then-bloated drummer. It was Moon's last appearance with the band. He died four months later.

---

**432.** a. Joe South
b. Neil Diamond
c. Phil Spector with Jeff Barry and Ellie Greenwich

**433.** What group started its chart career with four straight number 1 records, followed by two number 2s?

_____

**434.** Name five artists who recorded "Abraham, Martin and John."

_____

**435.** To what groups did the following belong before working under their own names?

a. Eddie Grant
b. Nils Lofgren
c. Billy Joel
d. Joan Jett
e. Bruce Springsteen
f. Tom Petty

433. The Jackson 5 hit number 1 with "I Want You Back," "ABC," "The Love You Save," and "I'll Be There" before slipping to number 2 with "Mama's Pearl" and "Never Can Say Goodbye."

434. Dion in 1968; the Miracles in 1969; Moms Mabley also in 1969; Tom Clay as part of a medley in 1971; and Ray Charles on his 1972 album *Message to the People.*

435.    a. The Equals            d. The Runaways
         b. Grin                  e. Steel Mill
         c. The Hassles         f. Mudcrutch

The Hassles, a Long Island (New York) bar band. The swarthy singer at left was an innocent man in 1984.

**436.** *Name seven groups with female drummers.*

**437.** *In 1967 the Beatles re-formed their company, Beatles Ltd., into Apple Corp. upon the advice of their tax experts. The idea was for the company to become a source of support and financing for all areas of creativity, including music, film-making, publishing, design, and electronics, but it was Apple Records that came closest to fulfilling the Beatles' goals. Which of the following recorded for Apple Records?*

a. *The Modern Jazz Quartet*
b. *Trash*
c. *Doris Troy*
d. *Richard Brautigan*
e. *Ronnie Spector*
f. *Hot Chocolate*
g. *Bill Elliot and the Electric Oz Band*

**438.** *The Italian Asphalt and Pavement Company had a number 97 "hit" in 1970 with their single "Check Yourself" before disappearing. Perhaps they should have stuck to the name they'd originally recorded under. What was it?*

**439.** *Keyboardist/vocalist Billy Preston is best known for his work as a sideman for Little Richard, Ray Charles, the Beatles, and the Rolling Stones. Name Billy Preston's famous mother.*

Honey Lantree, keeping the Honeycombs' swingin' beat.

**436.**  1. The Honeycombs     5. The Carpenters
       2. The Go-Go's            6. Velvet Underground
       3. Mojo Men             7. The Bangles
       4. The Belle Stars

---

**437.** They all did. Brautigan's contribution was a 1969 LP, *Listening to Richard Brautigan*, which included recitations of "Trout Fishing in America" and "The Pill Versus the Spring Hill Mine Disaster," among others. Ronnie Spector did one single, "Try Some, Buy Some"/"Tandoori Chicken," in 1971.

---

**438.** The Duprees, who are best known for their 1962 make-out favorite, "You Belong to Me."

---

**439.** Ernestine Wade. She played Sapphire in both the radio and TV versions of "Amos 'n' Andy."

**440.** *Before his successful career as one of the hottest heartland rockers of the eighties began, Donnie Iris was a schoolteacher in New Castle, Pennsylvania. Even earlier, however, Iris also sang lead on a 1970 hit. Name it and Iris's group at that time.*

**441.** *What is the family relationship of Bob Marley and Bunny Wailer?*

**442.** *What conspicuous difference exists between the 45 and LP versions of Fleetwood Mac's "Say You Love Me"?*

**443.** *Name the four keyboard players who played with Yes.*

**444.** *What famous rock & roll disc jockey got his professional start in his hometown, Caldwell, Idaho, and from there moved to Moscow (Idaho), Spokane, Seattle, San Bernardino, and Boston before landing in a city where he has become known as "Superjock"? What was his first job in that city?*

**440.** Donnie Iris was the voice of the Jaggerz, who scored with the proto-bubblegum hit "The Rapper."

---

**441.** According to Timothy White's Marley biography, *Catch a Fire*, Bob's mother lived with Bunny's pop. Bob and Bunny met Peter (McIn)Tosh while still schoolboys and formed the Wailers in the late sixties.

---

**442.** The single version, issued well after the album, has an overdubbed electric guitar. The record company presumably thought the song needed some extra punch, although in many cities the album cut was played anyway, and it seemed to do as well in sales.

---

**443.** Tony Kaye, Rick Wakeman, Patrick Moraz, and Geoff Downes.

---

**444.** The DJ is Larry Lujack, sarcastic morning man for WLS. His first job in Chicago was as all-night man for WCFL in 1967 for a few months before moving to WLS as afternoon man. In 1976, when WCFL went to a beautiful music/soft rock format, Lujack (who had since moved back to WCFL) remained with the station doing the non-rock format, but after some time at this he switched back to WLS and rock once more. In his 1975 book, *Superjock*, Lujack said, "DJ = Dumb Job."

**445.** Name two or more artists (groups or individuals) who had Top 40 hits with these songs.

a. "Rockin' Robin"
b. "Please Mr. Postman"
c. "Loco-Motion"
d. "I Heard It Through the Grapevine"
e. "Stay"
f. "Ain't Too Proud to Beg"
g. "Another Saturday Night"

h. "Barbara Ann"
i. "Do You Wanna Dance?"
j. "(I Know) I'm Losing You"
k. "Never Can Say Goodbye"
l. "Memphis"
m. "Light My Fire"
n. "We Can Work It Out"
o. "MacArthur Park"

**446.** With which singer, other than Art Garfunkel, did Paul Simon record a hit duet?

**447.** Name ten artists injured (or worse) in traffic mishaps.

**448.** Which of the following songs have Bruce Springsteen and the E Street Band never played live?

a. "Mony Mony"
b. "I'll Be Doggone"
c. "Macho Man"
d. "Dancing in the Street"
e. "Mountain of Love"
f. "Rendezvous"

g. "Hearts of Stone"
h. "Magic Bus"
i. "Santa Claus Is Coming to Town"
j. "Good Rockin' Tonight"

**445.**  a. Bobby Day, Michael Jackson
 b. The Marvelettes, The Carpenters
 c. Little Eva, Grand Funk Railroad
 d. Marvin Gaye, Gladys Knight and the Pips
 e. Maurice Williams and the Zodiacs, the Four Seasons, Jackson Browne
 f. The Temptations, The Rolling Stones
 g. Sam Cooke, Cat Stevens
 h. The Regents, The Beach Boys
 i. Bobby Freeman, The Beach Boys, Bette Midler
 j. The Temptations, Rare Earth, Rod Stewart
 k. The Jackson 5, Issac Hayes, Gloria Gaynor
 l. Lonnie Mack, Johnny Rivers
 m. The Doors, Jose Feliciano
 n. The Beatles, Stevie Wonder
 o. Richard Harris, Donna Summer

---

**446.** Phoebe Snow. They got together on "Gone at Last," which made the Top 40 in 1975.

---

**447.**  1. Bob Dylan
 2. Teddy Pendergrass
 3. Stevie Wonder
 4. Eddie Cochran
 5. Gene Vincent
 6. Billy Stewart
 7. Robert Plant
 8. Jeff Beck
 9. Duane Allman
 10. Berry Oakley

---

**448.** b, "I'll Be Doggone"; g, "Hearts of Stone" (even though Springsteen wrote it); and h, "Magic Bus" (he just stole the riff for "She's the One").

A psychedelic phantasmagoria, the Amboy Dukes, had a national hit in 1968 with "Journey to the Center of the Mind." Their lead guitarist (second from right) became one of the seventies' most flamboyant figures. That's Ted Nugent.

**449.** *Besides Tommy, star of his own rock opera, and Jimmy, the misguided protagonist of* Quadrophenia, *Pete Townshend created another character with five letters in his name: Bobby. But this individual never appeared, despite efforts on Townshend's part that led to a self-described "nervous breakdown." For what project was Bobby created, and what became of it?*

**450.** *From which previous bands did the four members of Bad Company come?*

**451.** *"TSOP" by MFSB topped the U.S. charts in 1974. What do these sets of initials stand for?*

**452.** *Name two artists who once made records distributed by Motown and went on to become major country/pop artists.*

**453.** *What was the first record released by Stiff Records?*

**449.** After the success of *Tommy*, Pete Townshend took his growing mystical, social, and technological hopes and fears and mixed them up in one multi-media science fiction project known as "Lifehouse." The story, set in a future without rock, was to take the performer/audience interaction Townshend felt onstage during *Tommy*'s "See Me, Feel Me" finale, explicate it, and make it permanent for the band and actors. But the logistics of renting a theater, filling it with people for at least six months, designing and using the latest sonic hardware, and levitating and dematerializing the whole shebang, not to mention attempting to explain the ball of confusion to uncomprehending associates, caused the collapse of the ambitious undertaking in 1971, bringing on the emotional exhaustion of its mastermind. Some songs from the period were salvaged and made into the landmark *Who's Next* album later that year. Others were fitted into *Quadrophenia*, appeared as singles, or turned up on Townshend solo LPs or Who compilations such as *Odds and Sods*.

**450.** Singer Paul Rodgers amd drummer Simon Kirke were from Free; guitarist Mick Ralphs emigrated from Mott the Hoople, and bassist Boz Burrell arrived from King Crimson (after spurning the Who).

**451.** "The Sound of Philadelphia" and Mother Father Sister Brother (although there are other theories on the latter).

**452.** Debby Boone and T. G. Sheppard.

**453.** "Heart of the City," by Nick Lowe. It was given the serial number BUY1 by Stiff, self-described as the world's most flexible record label. Lowe had been a member of Brinsley Schwarz, which was managed by Stiff co-founder Jake Riviera.

**454.** *To which of the following groups did Eric Clapton belong?*

    a. *The Yardbirds*
    b. *Delaney and Bonnie and Friends*
    c. *Derek and the Dominoes*
    d. *Savoy Brown*
    e. *War*
    f. *John Mayall's Bluesbreakers*
    g. *Fleetwood Mac*
    h. *Blind Faith*
    i. *Cream*

**455.** *The Move is best known for its 1972 mini-hit "Do Ya," the group's only U.S. chart record. The Move's leader had more success when the group evolved into a seven-man band. Name the later group.*

**456.** *What do Patti Smith, Meat Loaf, Hall and Oates, the New York Dolls, Tom Robinson, and Grand Funk Railroad have in common?*

**457.** *The Who began its 1973 U.S. tour at the Cow Palace in San Francisco. As always, Keith Moon sat behind the drum kit, ready to bash away during songs from the band's newest rock opus,* Quadrophenia, *and the usual selection of Who classics. However, Moon was forced to leave the stage before the show ended. What happened? Who replaced him?*

454. All but War (that was Eric Burdon), Savoy Brown, and Fleetwood Mac. Clapton participated in the formation of Cream, Blind Faith, and Derek and the Dominoes. (He was Derek.)

455. Electric Light Orchestra. Their first charted single, "Roll Over Beethoven," appeared in 1973.

456. Each has had an album produced by Todd Rundgren. Only Loaf's and Grand Funk's were hits.

457. Moon passed out twice onstage, victim (he claimed) of a drink spiked with the animal tranquilizer PCP. After the second collapse, Pete Townshend yelled out into the audience for a substitute, and nineteen-year-old Scott Halpin answered the call. Halpin, just arrived on the West Coast from Iowa, played three songs to finish the concert. Halpin's assessment of the experience: "I really admire [the band's] stamina. I only played three numbers and I was dead." Roger Daltrey said Halpin was a good player.

Patti Smith, 1976.

**458.** What do the following have in common: Lei'd in Hawaii, Add Some Music, Adult Child, *and* Landlocked.

_____

**459.** Who played the young W. C. Handy in the film St. Louis Blues *and* later recorded with the Beatles and Stones before cutting his own number 1 hits?

_____

**460.** Match the artists with the record labels they own.

a. Led Zeppelin            1. Dark Horse
b. The Moody Blues         2. Rocket
c. Elton John              3. Bludgeon Riffola
d. Pete Townshend          4. Threshold
e. Def Leppard             5. Swan Song
f. George Harrison         6. Eel Pie

_____

**461.** What late seventies New York band achieved its first success abroad with an updated (and sexually revised) version of an old Randy and the Rainbows number?

_____

**462.** What's the connection between Steely Dan and the Soft Machine?

_____

**463.** Reggae music replaced tourism as Jamaica's number-two industry in the seventies. What's number one?

_____

**464.** Who played John Lennon in the original Broadway production of Beatlemania?

_____

**465.** What duo has made the most number 1 records?

**458.** They are all unreleased Beach Boys albums, rejected for poor track selection, inferior recording, or both.

**459.** Billy Preston. The number 1 hits were 1973's "Will It Go Round in Circles" and "Nothing from Nothing" in 1974. Originally a gospel musician, Preston has returned to his roots and no longer records secular music.

**460.** a—5; b—4; c—2; d—6; e—3; f—1.

**461.** Blondie had its first high chart placement in England with "Denis" (in 1963 the Rainbows sang about "Denise") in 1978.

**462.** Both group names were inspired by novelist William Burroughs. *The Soft Machine* is the title of Burroughs's third novel. "Steely Dan" is the name of a dildo in his first, *Naked Lunch*.

**463.** Bauxite (for aluminum).

**464.** Marshall Crenshaw, who's gone on to a fine, non-clonelike recording career.

**465.** By the end of 1983 Hall and Oates had beat out the closest competition, the Everly Brothers, who'd had four number 1 singles. The Hall and Oates records include "Rich Girl" (1977); "Kiss on My List" (1981); "Private Eyes" (1981); "I Can't Go for That (No Can Do)" (1981); and "Maneater" (1982).

**466.** In 1978 producer Lorne Michaels publicly invited the Beatles to appear on NBC's "Saturday Night Live." How much money did he offer them?

**467.** What do Marc Bolan and Bing Crosby have in common?

**468.** Who sang about the following geographical spots?

    a. Paris
    b. Boston
    c. New York in the dead of winter
    d. London's Chelsea district
    e. Kingston, Jamaica
    f. Saigon
    g. Detroit
    h. Tulsa
    i. Cleveland
    j. Baltimore

**469.** This well-known composer had an entire album of his music recorded by another artist. Later he recorded with an ex-Beatle. Although he has been a successful recording performer, producer, and carouser, he's never appeared before an audience. Who is he?

**470.** Choose the correct wording of Jon Landau's famous Bruce Springsteen review:

    a. "I saw rock & roll future and its name is Bruce Springsteen."
    b. "I have seen the future of rock & roll and its name is Bruce Springsteen."
    c. "I have seen rock & roll's future and its name is Bruce Springsteen."

**466.** He offered $3,200 for the whole lot of them. George Harrison actually accepted the offer—and demanded $800, his share of the money.

**467.** Both died shortly after TV appearances with David Bowie. Crosby and Bowie taped a CBS Christmas special together in August 1977 and Crosby died the following October. Then Bowie taped an appearance with Bolan on the British series that his old rival, Bolan, was hosting. It was Bolan's last show; he died a few days later.

**468.**  a. Joni Mitchell ("A Free Man in Paris")
b. The Standells ("Dirty Water")
c. The Tradewinds ("New York's a Lonely Town")
d. Elvis Costello ("I Don't Want to Go to Chelsea")
e. The Wailers ("Trenchtown Rock") and Toots & The Maytals ("Country Roads")
f. Charlie Daniels ("Still in Saigon")
g. Fats Domino ("Detroit City Blues")
h. Eric Clapton ("Tulsa Time")
i. Ian Hunter ("Cleveland Rocks")
j. Randy Newman ("Baltimore")

**469.** Harry Nilsson, who has had three Top 10 hits, several Top 20 albums, and whose work has been recorded by Randy Newman, among others, also made the 1975 album *Pussycat* with producer John Lennon. Nilsson insisted that he could never approximate his studio sound live and so confined his public appearances to barhopping with such cronies as Ringo Starr and the late Keith Moon.

**470.** All are correct. But (a) is what Landau wrote in *The Real Paper*. Landau went on to become Springsteen's producer and manager (because he was correct).

In the forefront: Bruce Springsteen, Janis Ian, and Billy Joel.
Plus disc jockey and rock & roll fanatic Ed Sciaky.

*471.* *On his triumphant return to England in 1981, Bruce Spring-*
*steen figuratively "tore down the house" at each performance.*
*During his first visit to Britain in October of 1975, he almost*
*literally tore the house down at London's Hammersmith*
*Odeon. What caused the New Jersey rocker's rage?*

*472.* *What interesting effect can one obtain by playing a stereo rec-*
*ord after doing the following: 1. reversing the hot and ground*
*leads on one channel of the stereo phono cartridge; and 2.*
*throwing the "mono" switch on the stereo receiver/amp? Using*
*this process, on which Beatles song does John Lennon teach us*
*how to spell the word "home"? (The spelling lesson is not*
*audible by normal means but is loud and clear using this*
*technique.)*

231

471. The presence of posters and buttons at the gig reading "I Have Seen the Future of Rock." They were scheduled to be distributed by Columbia Records. Springsteen, tired of the charges of "hype" that followed the success of *Born to Run* in America, ordered the promotional giveaway scrapped. He began by ripping posters from the Odeon's walls.

---

472. What the activities described will lead to is playing a record out of phase, which cancels the information common to both channels. In other words, everything that was on both channels at equal volume in the stereo record will now be reduced to silence. The material that was on only a single channel will remain. Another way to look at it is that everything in the middle of the stereo listening field will disappear. This can lead to interesting results, such as instrumentals where there once were vocals (if the vocal parts were in the middle) or vice versa. A monaural record under these circumstances will theoretically cancel out completely and you will hear nothing at all, but in practice, there's always some imbalance, and some faint sounds are usually heard. Try this with Bruce Springsteen's *Born to Run* album. The title track sounds very different under these circumstances: The glockenspiel is especially prominent. The second cut of side two, "She's the One," is effectively mono and cancels out completely. The process of canceling the common material by rewiring the cartridge has sometimes been referred to as "out-of-phase stereo" (OOPS).

The spelling lesson is in the song "Ob La Di, Ob La Da." All through the song, John is in the background saying things, some of which come through even in the usual in-phase stereo. (For example—Paul: ". . . buys a twenty-carat diamond ring." John: "Ring!") The spelling lesson comes in the second chorus. With the out-of-phase wiring, Paul's and John's vocals are audible, but most of the music is canceled out. Paul says: "In a couple of years they will build a home sweet home. . . . " John contributes: "Home. H-O-M-E."

**473.** *For whom were the following songs written?*

a. "Wendy" (The Beach Boys)
b. "Our House" (Crosby, Stills and Nash)
c. "Layla" (Derek and the Dominoes)
d. "Shine on You Crazy Diamond" (Pink Floyd)
e. "Shannon" (Henry Gross)
f. "Oh Carol" (Neil Sedaka)
g. "You Never Give Me Your Money" (The Beatles)
h. "Here, My Dear" (Marvin Gaye)
i. "Only a Pawn in Their Game" (Bob Dylan)
j. "Happy Birthday" (Stevie Wonder)
k. "Of Missing Persons" (Jackson Browne)
l. "Blue" (Joni Mitchell)
m. "You're So Vain" (Carly Simon)
n. "He Was a Friend of Mine" (The Byrds)

---

**474.** *Who wrote songs about or addressed to the following?*

a. Johnny Carson
b. Bette Davis
c. Gene Vincent
d. Charles Starkweather (convicted murderer)
e. Abraham Lincoln, Martin Luther King, Jr., and John F. Kennedy
f. Otis Redding
g. Marilyn Monroe
h. Bobby Kennedy
i. Oswald Mosley (British fascist leader)
j. John Sinclair (pot activist, band manager)
k. Haile Selassie (Ethiopian emperor)
l. Neil Young
m. James Dean
n. Ayatollah Khomeini
o. Caryl Chessman (criminal and author executed in 1960)
p. Stephen Biko (South African poet)
q. Angela Davis

**473.**
a. Brian Wilson's daughter, Wendy
b. Joni Mitchell
c. Patti Boyd Harrison Clapton
d. Syd Barrett
e. Gross's dog, Shannon
f. Carole King
g. Allen Klein
h. Anna Gordy, his wife then
i. Medgar Evers
j. Martin Luther King, Jr.
k. Lowell George, late Little Feat guitarist
l. James Taylor
m. Warren Beatty, perhaps
n. Fred "Sonic" Smith (of the MC 5)

---

**474.**
a. Brian Wilson, "Johnny Carson"
b. Jackie DeShannon and Donna Weiss, "Bette Davis Eyes"
c. Ian Dury, "Sweet Gene Vincent"
d. Bruce Springsteen, "Nebraska"
e. Dick Feller, "Abraham, Martin and John"
f. Robby Krieger, "Running Blue"
g. Elton John, "Candle in the Wind"
h. David Crosby, "Long Time Gone"
i. Elvis Costello, "Less Than Zero"
j. John Lennon, "John Sinclair"
k. Bob Marley, "Jah Live"
l. Ronnie Van Zant, "Sweet Home Alabama"
m. Glenn Frey and Don Henley, "James Dean"
n. The Clash, "Rock the Casbah"
o. Ronnie Hawkins, "The Ballad of Caryl Chessman"
p. Peter Gabriel, "Biko"
q. John Lennon, "Angela"

**475.** *The Band invited virtually all the musicians they had ever played with to appear with them in the 1978 film* The Last Waltz. *Why was Ringo Starr included?*

_____

**476.** *What did Jeff Beck, Tim Bogert, and Carmine Appice have in common before forming the group Beck, Bogert, and Appice?*

_____

**477.** *During the spring of 1970, songs by White Plains, Edison Lighthouse, and the Pipkins all made the national Top 15. What interesting sound did these three songs share?*

_____

**478.** *What current E Street Band members got their jobs through a newspaper ad?*

_____

**479.** *What legendary Southern boogie band recorded a musical version of Edgar Allan Poe's "The Bells" during its early incarnation as a California-based psychedelic group?*

_____

**480.** *Who invented the air guitar?*

_____

**481.** *Why can it be said that Richard Hell is the logical successor to Rod McKuen?*

_____

**482.** *Who is listed in* The Guinness Book of World Records *as the loudest band?*

**475.** The Band played on "Sunshine Life for Me (Sail Away Raymond)," a song written by George Harrison that appears on Ringo's most successful solo LP, *Ringo*.

---

**476.** Bogert and Appice recorded Holland/Dozier/Holland's "You Keep Me Hangin' On" in 1967 when they were members of Vanilla Fudge. Jeff Beck recorded the song at Motown in 1972.

---

**477.** All three were studio-only groups that featured the voice of Tony Burrows singing lead.

---

**478.** Drummer Max Weinberg and pianist Roy Bittan answered a musicians' classified in the *Village Voice* in the summer of 1974 and were hired immediately.

---

**479.** The Allman Brothers.

---

**480.** We all did, but Joe Cocker was the first to be paid for playing it.

---

**481.** Both are published poets. Additionally, Richard Hell's anthemic "Blank Generation" is actually a minor rewrite of "Beat Generation," which appears on McKuen's Brunswick album *Songs Our Mummy Taught Us*. Sample lyrics: "I belong to the beat generation/And I don't let anything trouble my mind." George Harrison lost a lot of money for a lot less.

---

**482.** That's right.

# 8

# *Synthpop And Michaelmania*
## (The Eighties)

483. *Who are Jeffrey Hyman, Thomas Erdelyi, Douglas Colvin, Mark Bell, and John Cummings?*

484. *According to* The Guinness Book of World Records, *who is the most successful composer of all time?*

485. *Why did Johnny Rotten change his name back to John Lydon—and then to Rotten again?*

486. *How many solo LPs has Michael Jackson recorded?*

487. *Jackson's* Thriller *LP included seven Top 10 singles. Name them, and for extra credit, name their B sides.*

**483.** The Ramones.

---

**484.** Paul McCartney. When he was given the award by Guinness in 1979, McCartney had written forty-three songs that had sold more than a million copies each. Also the world's most successful recording artist, he had sold 10 million albums and 100 million singles as of that time. "Yesterday" is the most recorded song in history, with more than 1,200 versions registered. All of which, needless to say, makes McCartney extremely wealthy. He was recently cited as the richest man in show business, and estimates of his income have him earning as much as $100,000 a day.

---

**485.** The alleged reason for the name change was Rotten/Lydon's desire to disassociate himself from the Sex Pistols circus and establish an identity outside of the Malcolm McLaren-produced hype. In the early days of Public Image Ltd., he became very angry if someone referred to him as Rotten. However, it turned out that McLaren claimed ownership of the name Johnny Rotten, and when the two split, McLaren refused to let Lydon (the name Johnny was born with) use the name. After a court case in the summer of 1983, Lydon got Rotten again.

---

**486.** Five: *Got to Be There* (1972), *Ben* (1972), *Off the Wall* (1979), *E.T. the Extra Terrestrial* (1982), and *Thriller* (1982).

---

**487.** 1. "Beat It"/"Get on the Floor"
2. "Billie Jean"/"Can't Get Out of the Rain"
3. "The Girl Is Mine"/"Can't Get Out of the Rain"
4. "Thriller"/"Can't Get Out of the Rain"
5. "Wanna Be Startin' Somethin' "/instrumental of "Wanna Be Startin' Somethin' "
6. "Human Nature"/"Baby Be Mine"
7. "P.Y.T. (Pretty Young Thing)"/"Working Day and Night"

Talking Heads.

**488.** *The Talking Heads' "Swamp" appears on the sound track of two 1983 films. However, the song can be heard in only one of the films. Which one?*

---

**489.** *"Sheer torture. Dreadful. It's a waste of vinyl." This was a songwriter's verdict on versions of his songs that appeared on a platinum-selling LP. Name the speaker and the album he was talking about.*

---

**490.** *From which countries do these acts originate?*

a. Golden Earring      f. Olivia Newton-John
b. Abba      g. Musical Youth
c. Men at Work      h. Giorgio Moroder
d. The Stray Cats      i. Split Enz
e. Bryan Adams      j. Los Lobos

488. Although "Swamp" is included on the *King of Comedy* sound track LP, the song was edited out of that film. It does provide the background music for the "whorehouse" scene in *Risky Business.*

489. Elvis Costello gave that description of Linda Rondstadt's versions of "Party Girl," "Talking in the Dark," and "Girl's Talk." He was reported to have refused royalties from the sale of Ronstadt's album *Mad Love.*

490.
a. Holland  
b. Sweden  
c. Australia  
d. United States  
e. Canada  

f. Australia  
g. England  
h. Germany  
i. New Zealand  
j. United States  

The Stray Cats.

**491.** *What is the longest single ever to hit the British Top 10, an American record never even played on Top 40 radio in the United States, to our knowledge?*

**492.** *What well-known funk performer and studio musician is the son of seminal jazz figure Jimmy Heath?*

**493.** *On September 19, 1981, more than 400,000 people went to Washington D.C. for the AFL-CIO's Solidarity Day demonstration. On the same day, a veteran act drew even more people to a concert in Central Park. Who was it?*

**494.** *Which seventies group contained both Kid Creole and Coatimundi, and what are their real names?*

**495.** *Why was Pink Floyd's "Another Brick in the Wall" banned in South Africa?*

**496.** *Toni Basil, whose hit "Mickey" was a number 1 song in 1982, was the assistant choreographer for what classic rock film?*

**497.** *Name two famous British groups that have drummers named Roger Taylor.*

491. "The Crown," by Gary Byrd, which, despite its length of 10:35, hit the British Top 10 in the summer of 1983. (Eat your heart out, Don McLean.) Byrd's record, released by Motown on Stevie Wonder's Wondirection label, is a rap history of black culture.

492. (James) Mtume of "Juicy Fruit" fame.

493. Simon and Garfunkel. Does this prove that while union makes us strong, reunion makes us stronger?

494. Dr. Buzzard's Original "Savannah" Band was also led by August Darnell and Andy Hernandez.

495. Black school children adopted the song as an anthem in their struggle against the apartheid school system. ("We don't need no education," they sang.. "We don't need no thought control.") On May 2, 1980, South African authorities forbade the playing of the song on the grounds that it was "prejudicial to the safety of the state."

496. *The T.A.M.I. Show*, which makes the idea of Basil's record as "new music" farcical. The best dancing in the film, however, had nothing to do with Basil. James Brown made up his own steps.

497. Queen and Duran Duran.

**498.** In perhaps the oddest personnel changeover in rock history, which "dinosaur" progressive band joined forces with the pop brains behind the lightweight British hit "Video Killed the Radio Star"?

_____

**499.** When the original Animals got together in 1983 for their first full-fledged reunion tour after seventeen years, a former member of Eric Burdon's New Animals was topping the U.S. album and singles charts with his current group. Name this guitar player.

_____

**500.** What do the eighties' most notorious badass punk funker, Rick James, and old folkie-turned-multimedia-experimentalist Neil Young have in common?

_____

**501.** In 1983, on the eve of the twentieth anniversary of the Beatles' precedent-shattering "Ed Sullivan Show" appearances, which former Fab Four member was without a U.S. record deal?

_____

**502.** Where did Duran Duran get that name?

_____

**503.** What was David Byrne and Chris Frantz's first band?

_____

**504.** The 1971–74 incarnation of Jonathan Richman's Modern Lovers contained two members who went on to join more successful bands. Who were they?

**498.** Yes, at the end of the line in 1980, added former Buggles Geoff Downes and Trevor Horn to replace departed guitarist Steve Howe and vocalist Jon Anderson. The group went on to massive success in 1983–84 with "Owner of a Lonely Heart."

**499.** Andy Summers, who, with the Police, was riding high with "Every Breath You Take" and *Synchronicity*.

**500.** James and Young were in the Mynah Birds, a mid-sixties band, together. The Mynahs had a contract with but never recorded for James's current label, Motown. One reason they never recorded was that the draft system was after James. (Young, as a Canadian, didn't have that worry, and so headed west.)

**501.** Ringo Starr, whose *Old Wave* LP came out in Canada and Europe in 1983 but made it to America only as an import.

**502.** From a character in the 1968 Jane Fonda film *Barbarella*.

**503.** The Artistics, a.k.a. the Autistics, was formed at the Rhode Island School of Design. This first edition of the Talking Heads, a trio with Tina Weymouth on bass, first performed in 1976 as the opening act for the Ramones.

**504.** Guitarist Jerry Harrison, who joined the Talking Heads in February 1977; and Dave Robinson, who joined the Cars the same year.

**505.** *What do Michael Jackson and Lesley Gore have in common?*

_____

**506.** *When Del Shannon reappeared in the Top 40 in 1982, almost seventeen years had passed since his last hit. It had been almost nineteen years since another rock & roll singer's last Top 40 hit when he finally re-entered the charts in 1981. Who was he, and what was his 1981 hit?*

_____

**507.** *After an eleven-year absence, which Motown group returned to the fold during the label's twenty-fifth anniversary year?*

Quincy Jones.

**505.** Both have had records produced by Quincy Jones. Jones produced Gore's early sixties hits, including "It's My Party," and he's made both of Jackson's Epic solo LPs.

---

**506.** When Gary "U.S." Bonds hit with "This Little Girl" in 1981, it had been almost nineteen years since "Seven Day Weekend," which made number 27 in 1962. Del Shannon's 1982 "Sea of Love" marked the first time in the Top 40 for him since "Stranger in Town," number 30 in 1965. Both recent hits were produced by modern-day rock & roll artists, Bonds' by Bruce Springsteen and Del Shannon's by Tom Petty.

---

**507.** The Four Tops came back to Berry Gordy's label in 1983 after recording stints at ABC Records and Casablanca.

**508.** *This drummer and bass player combined to form a powerful rhythm section on Pete Townshend's solo records,* Empty Glass *and* All the Best Cowboys Have Chinese Eyes. *Afterwards they teamed up with two Scottish guitarists to create one of 1983's most critically acclaimed new bands. Name the musicians and the group.*

**509.** *What is* Emotional Facism?

**510.** *What is the origin of the band UB40's name?*

**511.** *The Clash takes its politics seriously, a stance that often gets its members into difficulties with their record company and, sometimes, the law. In 1977 bassist Paul Simonon and current drummer Topper Headon were arrested, an event that inspired "Jail Guitar Doors," a tribute to other musicians who had heard the iron bars slammed behind them. What was Simonon and Headon's crime?*

**512.** *What was the first video to appear on MTV?*

**513.** *Who was the first artist to simultaneously have the number 1 pop single and LP and the number 1 black single and LP?*

**514.** *What band was voted the most popular in the Soviet Union in 1982?*

**508.** Drummer Mark Brzezicki and bassist Tony Butler joined forces with Bruce Watson and Stuart Adamson to assemble Big Country. The quartet, whose debut album, *The Crossing*, was recorded with noted producer Steve Lillywhite, found immediate success on both sides of the Atlantic with the singles "In a Big Country" and "Fields of Fire."

**509.** Elvis Costello's original title for his third album, actually titled *Armed Forces*. The LP's music makes the original concept pretty clear.

**510.** UB40 is the British unemployment form.

**511.** Shooting racing pigeons that belonged to someone in the neighborhood of the recording studio where the band was working. Simonon and Headon were playing with air guns, aiming at the pigeons, when they were spied by police in a helicopter who thought they'd come upon a group of terrorists. Part of their trial and its attendant hoopla can be seen in the 1980 film *Rude Boy*.

**512.** "Video Killed the Radio Star," by the Buggles. The date was not December 7, 1941, but August 1, 1981, but it too shall live in infamy.

**513.** Michael Jackson, for *Thriller*, in 1983. The single in question is "Billie Jean."

**514.** Uriah Heep, according to *Billboard*. (Here, James Watt, is a real argument against socialism.)

**515.** *What single spent the most consecutive weeks on the Top 100?*

_____

**516.** *Which of the following was never a rock critic or journalist?*

    *a. Chrissie Hynde*         *d. David Byrne*
    *b. Patti Smith*            *e. Mark Knopfler*
    *c. Pete Townshend*

_____

**517.** *Miles Copeland, Sr., was the chief CIA agent in Egypt and Lebanon during the fifties and sixties. His oldest son, Miles, Jr., formed IRS Records. His youngest, Stewart, is the drummer of the Police. What occupation did his middle son, Ian, find for himself?*

_____

**518.** *Not only are the Thompson Twins not twins—in fact, not even related—there aren't two of them, but three. Where did they get their damn name, then?*

The Pretenders, alive and kicking.

515. Soft Cell's "Tainted Love." In 1982, after 43 consecutive weeks on the charts, it beat out Paul Davis's "I Go Crazy," which had been on for 40 straight weeks in 1977–78.

516. Byrne, one of the most literate rockers ever, nevertheless has never written anything so mercenary as a record review. Hynde contributed to the British pop papers when she first moved to England; Smith was a frequent contributor to both *Creem* and *Rolling Stone* in the early seventies; Knopfler was a reporter for his hometown newspaper; Townshend wrote a column for *Melody Maker* in the early seventies and is now an editor for the British publishing house Faber and Faber.

517. Ian Copeland runs the F.B.I. (Frontier Booking International) talent agency, which books rock concert tours for the Police, among others.

518. From the very popular European comic books *Tin Tin*.

**519.** *Name ten musicians who recorded with the Clash before the expulsion of Mick Jones.*

_____

**520.** *Before she became the sensation of 1984, Cyndi Lauper recorded with a New York-based quintet. Name the group.*

_____

**521.** *Identify the combination that has never appeared on the same record:*

   a. *Bruce Springsteen and Ronnie Spector*
   b. *Mick Ronson and T-Bone Burnett*
   c. *Chrissie Hynde and Ray Davies*
   d. *Lou Reed and Steve Winwood*
   e. *Luther Vandross and John Lennon*

**519.** Jones, Joe Strummer, Paul Simonon, and Tory Crimes appeared on the group's first album. Nicky "Topper" Headon soon replaced Crimes. On *London Calling*, Mickey Gallagher (organ), the otherwise unenumerated Irish Horns and whistler Baker Glare augmented the basic lineup. *Sandinista* had a cast of dozens, including Gallagher, Tymon Dogg, Norman Watt-Roy, J. P. Nicholson, Ellen Foley, David Payne, Ray Gasconne, Band Sgt. Dave Yates, Den Hegarty, Luke, Ben, and Maria Gallagher, Gary and Bill Barnacle, Jody Winscott, Ivan Julien, Noel Tempo Bailey, Anthony Nelson Steelie, Lew Lewis, Gerald Baxter-Warman, Terry McQuade, Rudolf Adolphus Jordan and Mikey Dread. On *Combat Rock*, the group once again slimmed down but still used backing vocalists Foley, Allen Ginsberg, Joe Ely, and Futura 2000, plus keyboardists Dogg and Poly Mandell and saxman Gary Barnacle.

**520.** Lauper's first group was Blue Angel, which recorded a self-titled album for Polydor in 1980, produced by Roy Halee (best-known for his work with Simon and Garfunkel). Blue Angel keyboardist/saxophonist John Turi co-wrote "Witness," from *She's So Unusual*, with Lauper.

**521.** Hynde and Davies created a child together but they never made a record together. Of the others, Springsteen and Spector matched up on Bruce's "You Mean So Much to Me Baby," which Miami Steve produced as an Epic single for Southside Johnny in 1976; Ronson and Burnett played together on Bob Dylan's *Hard Rain;* Winwood, believe it or not, played keyboards on Reed's *Berlin;* while Vandross and Lennon were both sidemen on David Bowie's *Young Americans*.

**522.** *According to* Rolling Stone *and some other pundits, Journey is among rock's most faceless bands. However, 'twas not always thus for its band members. Name the bands in which Journey's original lineup got its start. (To make it easy for the uninitiated, that lineup was: Gregg Rolie, keyboards and vocals; Neal Schon, guitar; George Tickner, guitar; Ross Valory, bass; Prairie Prince, drums.)*

**523.** *Name the "Boy" crazy singer who grew up in the same Gary, Indiana, neighborhood as the Jacksons.*

**524.** *Which of the following groups features no women?*

a. *The Thompson Twins*
b. *Culture Club*
c. *The Tom Tom Club*
d. *Gang of Four*
e. *ABC*
f. *Bruce Springsteen and the E Street Band*

**525.** *Which of the following groups is not racially integrated?*

a. *The E Street Band*
b. *War*
c. *Talking Heads*
d. *Madness*
e. *Big Country*

**522.** With the exception of Tickner, who was just starting his career, Journey's members had a checkered, all-but-illustrious list of credentials at the start. Rolie and Schon both played in early editions of Santana, Valory was part of the group with which Steve Miller made *Rock Love* in 1971, and Dunbar had played with both John Mayall's Bluesbreakers and Frank Zappa's Mothers of Invention.

**523.** Deniece Williams ("Let's Hear It for the Boy"). Her pre-teen vocal groups competed against Michael and his brothers in talent contests.

**524.** ABC.

**525.** The Talking Heads. The group often appears with black musicians as sidemen, but it is composed of four Caucasians.

# 9

# *The Harder They Come*
## (For Extra Credit)

**526.** Dick Orkin, longtime producer of funny and witty commercials for radio, first came to prominence in Cleveland, then moved to Chicago in the mid-sixties. While at WCFL in Chicago in 1965, he produced a series as a takeoff on the then-popular "Batman" TV series. Orkin's series was so successful that it continued through more than 180 daily episodes and generated at least one LP. What was this popular radio series of the sixties?

---

**527.** The song "Happiness Is," heard on TV for years as a Kent cigarettes commercial, was written by a singer who had several rock & roll hits in the early sixties. Who was he? What hits did he also write for the Kalin Twins and for Bobby Vinton?

526.  Orkin's dry humor soon took the "Chickenman" series far beyond mere parody. Orkin and two other WCFL employees, Jane Roberts and Jim Runyon, did most of the voices, including such characters as Benton Harbor (Chickenman), the Mayor of Midland City (a thinly disguised Chicago), and the Mayor's secretary, Honor Helfinger. Chickenman can still be heard fighting crime and/or evil on the LP *The Best of Chickenman* (Atco 33-207).

---

527.  The singer was Paul Evans, who, after the 1959 hit "Seven Little Girls Sitting in the Back Seat," hit with "Midnight Special" and "Happy-Go-Lucky Me" and came close with "The Brigade of Broken Hearts" in 1960. Evans also wrote "When" for the Kalin Twins and "Roses Are Red" for Bobby Vinton.

**528.** *A well-known disc jockey was heard during the sixties in Buffalo and then moved to late night on WLS in Chicago. He was also co-writer of "The Green Mosquito," a hit by the Tune Rockers in 1958. Who was he, and what record did he produce in Buffalo in 1959 that became a minor hit in Canada?*

_____

**529.** *What is electronically rechanneled stereo?*

_____

**530.** *One of the top records of 1963 was recorded by a father and his four sons, the Maligmat family, who came to the United States from the Philippines. Papa Doroteo Maligmat had for twenty years been a popular bandleader, earning the nickname "the Glenn Miller of Hong Kong." What was their first hit, and what did this group call itself?*

_____

**531.** *Joe Barry was a New Orleans-based singer who had one hit in 1961. The song he recorded was written in the forties by one T. Daffan and was made into a hit in 1954 by Les Paul and Mary Ford. He brought it back for the third time (after Oscar Black recorded the song, also in 1961). What was his hit, and what was the most striking thing about the Joe Barry version?*

**528.** The disc jockey was Art Roberts. Roberts did some production work in Buffalo in the late fifties, which led to his association with the Tune Rockers. He also put out at least two records on his own label, A.R.P. (for Art Roberts Productions). One of these, "First Sign of Love" by Billy Lehmann and the Penn-Men, showed little activity locally but, unbeknownst to Roberts, was picked up by a small Canadian label and made the CHUM Top 40 in Toronto. For most of the sixties, Robert's show from 9 P.M. to midnight on WLS in Chicago could be heard throughout most of the midwestern states.

**529.** Electronically rechanneled (reprocessed, altered, simulated, etc.) stereo is fake stereo. A mono master is electronically tampered with to make it appear that there are two separate channels, most of the time by using frequency separation (bass on one channel and treble on the other), adding reverb to one channel, using balance changes between channels, delaying one channel relative to the other, or using some combination of these gimmicks. The results, while not *invariably* awful, generally distort the original sound concept of the recording. Chuck Berry's rechanneled records are a perfect example of the atrocities that result from such tampering—they're awful in anything but mono.

**530.** They called themselves the Rocky Fellers and, in addition to the Top 20 "Killer Joe," also placed another record on the Top 100, "Like the Big Guys Do."

**531.** The song was "I'm a Fool to Care." On his record, Barry sounded like Fats Domino's clone.

**532.**  What is unusual about the sound of the original pressings of Fats Domino's "Blueberry Hill" on Imperial?

**533.**  What links these songs? "To Know Him Is to Love Him," the Teddy Bears; "My Sweet Lord," George Harrison; "Play with Fire," the Rolling Stones; and "On Broadway," the Drifters.

**534.**  In February 1967 a Chicago rock group reached the number 1 spot on Billboard's Top 100. What were the song and the group, and what was ironic about the group's showing on its hometown charts?

**535.**  The stereo versions of Del Shannon's "Hey! Little Girl," Patti Page's "Old Cape Cod," and Andy Williams's "Lonely Street" all have a similar flaw compared to their respective 45 versions. What is it?

**536.**  (Note: The following question is only for the most exacting stereo fanatics.) What is the difference between the stereo versions of "I Fought the Law" by the Bobby Fuller Four on the original Mustang LP and on Oldies but Goodies, Vol. 9?

532.    The single version has a tape slip in the middle of the song, causing part of the instrumental break to be distorted. This distortion was corrected in later pressings and on LPs, so today it is difficult to find the 45 as originally pressed.

---

533.    Phil Spector performed on each.

---

534.    The record was "Kind of a Drag," by the Buckinghams. Surprisingly, although it made number 1 nationally with the song, the group couldn't reach number 1 in its hometown, topping out at number 2 on the WLS Top 40 and at number 3 on the WCFL chart.

---

535.    The mono singles of all of these hits feature double-tracked lead vocals. The double tracking was probably done as the mono master was being made for the single, since none of the stereo versions have the overdubbed voice.

---

536.    It is the same mix, but the channels are reversed, left to right.

**537.** Count to twenty-one using song and album titles recorded by the following artists. (Example: Buffalo Springfield recorded "Uno Mundo."

1. Buffalo Springfield
2. The Beach Boys
3. ZZ Top
4. Jim Reeves
5. Dolly Parton
6. Bob Dylan
7. John Entwistle
8. The Beatles
9. The Clovers
10. The Yardbirds
11. The Grateful Dead
12. Bob Dylan
13. Seatrain
14. Love
15. David Bowie
16. Sam Cooke
17. The Four Seasons
18. Alice Cooper
19. The Rolling Stones
20. Eddie Cochran
21. The Rolling Stones

537.
1. "**Uno** Mundo"
2. "Little **Deuce** Coupe"
3. *Tres Hombres*
4. "**Four** Walls"
5. "**9 to 5**"
6. "From a Buick **Six**"
7. "Cell Number **7**"
8. "**Eight** Days a Week"
9. *Riot in Cell Block #9*
10. "**10** Little Indians"
11. *The Eleven*
12. "Rainy Day Women **#12** and 35"
13. "**13** Questions"
14. "**7 and 7** Is"
15. "TVC **15**"
16. "Only **Sixteen**"
17. "Opus **17** (Don't You Worry 'Bout Me)"
18. "**Eighteen**"
19. "**19**th Nervous Breakdown"
20. "**Twenty** Flight Rock"
21. "**2120** South Michigan Avenue"

# 10

# *The Long And Winding Road*
## (Essay Questions & Contest)

The ten authors of the best answers to any five of the following ten questions get free one-year subscriptions to *Rock & Roll Confidential*. All entries become the property of *Rock & Roll Confidential* and must be postmarked before midnight, December 31, 1986. Send entries to *Rock & Roll Confidential*, Department R, Box 1073, Maywood, NJ 07607.

---

1. *Plan an ideal Battle of the Bands. Four groups are playing. Who wins, what songs do they play, and why do they beat out the opposition?*

2. *Who is the most underrated figure in rock history? You can choose someone whose influence has never been properly acknowledged or an artist who has never gotten his or her just rewards and remains underappreciated. For the neglected influence, give examples of artists who have carried on his or her tradition. For the unappreciated musician, make a case so stirring that we'll run out and buy a record, assuming there is one.*

3. *You've finally gotten the chance to play DJ. You've got a forty-five-minute cassette on which to put your choices for the ultimate dance tape. The tape can't be any longer than 45 minutes, so keep running times in mind. List and explain the contents of your tape.*

4. *Describe the differences among punk, new wave, and new music and chart their evolution (or devolution) from 1976 to today.*

5. *Name five groups that could better serve the annals of rock by breaking up. Give convincing arguments for letting sleeping dogs lie.*

6. *Refute or defend the argument that the English take the best of American music and make it even better.*

7. *What are the greatest rock & roll lyrics ever written? Justify and explain your choice.*

8. *Why is home taping of prerecorded music a bad thing? Why is the practice harmless? Defend one of these propositions.*

_____

9. *Describe how rock and/or human history would have been different if one of the following were still alive: Buddy Holly; Sam Cooke; Alan Freed; Stuart Sutcliffe; Sid Vicious.*

_____

10. *Why did Michael Jackson use the song "Can't Get Out of the Rain" as the B side of three separate singles? Your answer can and should include mercenary, religious, and psychological speculations.*

# About The Authors

**Dave Marsh** was a founding editor of *Creem*, a music critic at *Newsday*, and an editor of *The Real Paper* in Boston before joining *Rolling Stone* as an associate editor in 1975. His column "American Grandstand" has appeared first in *Rolling Stone* and then in *Record*. His books include *Born to Run: The Bruce Springsteen Story*, *The Book of Rock Lists*, *The Rolling Stone Record Guide*, *Elvis*, and *Before I Get Old: The Story of the Who*. Marsh's record reviews are syndicated in more than 200 newspapers. He currently publishes a monthly rock and politics newsletter, *Rock & Roll Confidential*. A collection of his magazine and newspaper articles, *Fortunate Son*, will be published in 1985.

**Sandra Choron** has worked as an editor for eight years, at Hawthorn Books and Dell Publishing, specializing in popular culture and music. She was the editor of *The Book of Rock Lists* and now heads her own independent book producing and agenting firm, March Tenth, Inc. She is the author of *Class Reunion—The Photonovel* and co-author (with Edward Malca) of *Everybody's Investment Book*. She has recently completed work on *The Big Book of Kids' Lists*, which will be published in 1985, and is an associate editor of *Rock & Roll Confidential*.

**Debbie Geller** has written for *Record, Musician*, the *Observer*, and the syndicated radio program "Rock Quiz" and was contributor to *The Book of Rock Lists* and *The Rolling Stone Record Guide*. She is the co-author (with Arthur Geller) of *Living Longer and Loving It*. Ms. Geller is an associate editor of *Rock & Roll Confidential*.

# Index

274

275

# *Song Index*